VIETNAMESE
Food

R&R PUBLICATIONS MARKETING PTY LTD

CONTENTS

the land
AND ITS PEOPLE

Status	People's Socialist Republic
Area	329,565 sq km
Population	66,200,000
Language	Vietnamese
Religion	Buddhist.
Currency	Dong
National Day	September 2

Food for all moods

On a cold, blustery morning in a narrow, muddied, unsealed, suburban street in Hanoi, the capital of Vietnam, buyers and sellers of vegetables, fruit and flowers and food hawkers huddled under canvas awnings shading shadowy shops. While it was hot in the country's south, here, in the north, sheltered from pelting rain, a woman ignited a huge wad of newspapers. Tossing sections towards the road, she shouted, waving a mini-inferno.

I wondered if perhaps she had gone mad, a modern-day victim of more than 2,000 years in which war-torn Vietnam had struggled to expel foreign demons and cope with its own violent rebellions. My young interpreter, Mai grasped my hand. She, with fellow students, Tek, and male Hanh, would deliver me (a pillion-passenger) with the elan of Evel Knieval, on motorbikes daily through the city's insane traffic. This was so I could become, I believe, the first western woman to take a professional (crash) tertiary cooking course with Madame Do Minh Thu at Caoson College of Learning. The college is one of Hanoi's five university campuses.

Mai said:'The seller fans the fire to highlight her vegetables.' Then, Mai and Tek bought prolifically from the flame-thrower and other vendors. At Mai's family's pencil-narrow, three-storey home, designed to give maximum vegetable garden space (as in the style of many city houses), the girls prepared a procession of dishes while squatting on the kitchen floor. This is typical as most kitchens are tiny, with negligible bench space, a reason why many Vietnamese cook and eat out on the streets. Three invisible food gods presided over the nervous chefs. They had learned to cook only from their mothers.

Until recently, all Vietnamese girls were expected to prove culinary skills to a future husband's family before marriage; they still do in some villages. Mai and Tet will be assets for future in-laws.

Fluffy, long-grain rice steamed in a rice cooker (a more respected appliance than a refrigerator). Sticky or glutinous rice is usually reserved for desserts and special festival food but is often spiced and served for breakfast, wrapped in banana leaves. The world's biggest exporter of rice, next to America and Thailand, Vietnam has dozens of varieties of rice. Rice (cooked unwashed without salt) appears as rice flour, food-wrapping paper, powder, noodles, vermicelli, wine, vinegar and dubious moonshine.

Professional cooking courses are relatively new to Vietnam. In recent years visitors have taken short, more westernised courses in the 1901-built, grand Metropole Hotel in Hanoi, as well as in other hotels and restaurants in Hanoi and Saigon. I recommend three days to explore northern and southern Vietnamese cooking styles. The climate and fresh, colourful produce in each region has a strong influence on cooking styles. There is also a distinctive central region cuisine which was developed in the former imperial courts of Hue and also in the French-influenced old port of Hoi An.

Dominated by China from 200 BC, Vietnam inherited legacies of metal ploughs, irrigation systems, beasts of burden, chopsticks, Buddhism (hence vegetarianism), verbal recipes, table manners and, most importantly, rice cultivation.

am

Cattle accompanied 10th century Mongol herdsmen and Hanoi gave birth to Vietnam's national dish, *pho* (pronounced fur) which is beef soup, thick with noodles.

Thai traditions filtered into Vietnam at about the time the Portuguese missionaries introduced spices and Christianity to Thailand in the 14th century. Cambodia had Indian infusions, such as coffee, which filtered through to Vietnam. Coffee plants now cover Vietnam's countryside, which was formerly devastated by bomb blasts. The Vietnamese are also fond of curries.

The French occupied Vietnam from 1859 to 1954. Their imprint on Vietnamese cuisine remains. The French influence ranges from the introduction of produce such as wine, avocados, tomatoes, asparagus, corn, baguettes, pâté, salads, pastries, cafe au lait, cakes and ice cream, to the cooking method of sautéing.

The result of all these cultural influences is a rich array of tastes and traditions. Vietnamese food is not as spicy as Thai but is crisper, nor is it like Chinese cuisine as soy sauce is used less. Experts acknowledge that the peasant cuisines of China, France and Thailand are the world's best but having eaten my way from Hanoi to Ho Chi Minh City, I believe Vietnamese cuisine is the most exciting on earth. The secret is in *nuoc cham*, a pungent fish sauce. *Nuoc cham* is to the Vietnamese what soy is to the Chinese and Japanese, shrimp paste to Indonesians and *nam prik* (chilli sauce) is to the Thais. Fermented from anchovies, *nuoc cham* replaces salt in dishes and combines well with all meats and fish. Add lime juice, garlic, fresh, red chilli (sans seeds), sugar and vinegar, to taste, and it becomes *nuoc cham*, Vietnam's favourite dipping sauce, found on every table.

land AND ITS

What is an S-Bend?

It's not the design of a toilet (and there are few for the public in Vietnam). S is the shape of the country, reflected in the physiques of many of its 70- or so million people, including 54 different ethnic groups.

Envisage on a map a head raised in survival, a thin spine curved under the heavy burden of a bamboo pole yoke (*don ganh*) balanced on frail shoulders with each end of the bamboo pole holding a big basket containing anything from bananas to bricks. In the middle of the map, some vendors carry cooking braziers, bowls, chopsticks and drinks for instant serving to street patrons. A knee is bent on the metaphoric map of Vietnam. In the far south, including the Mekong Delta, the map resembles a foot, poised ready to repel adversaries into the Gulf of Thailand.

An S-bend is the national highway winding from north to south for about 1,600 km along the Indochinese Peninsula in a massed area a bit bigger than Italy (which also has an aggressive foot in its south). The highway is a paradoxical good-bad way to traverse Vietnam by bus. In seasons of monsoons and typhoons the road is subject to flooding and mudslides and is pot-holed and sometimes terrifying. A train runs but at night visitors miss the stunning beauty of the countryside. Through bus windows, one sees an endless lake of rice paddies punctuated by the conical hats of women working. Running past shark-toothed mountains, the bus affords views of the Gulf of Tonkin and the South China Sea.

The countryside is dotted with waterfalls, rain forests, lagoons, groves of coconut palms and other tropical fruit trees. Cattle, water buffalo and goats graze in pastures. There are intriguing and depressed towns (all advertising photocopying facilities) and an increasing number of resorts.

The climate in Vietnam is varied, from northern cold in winter, to a hot dry summer, to southern humidity. The central mountains, where the French built hill stations, provide respite from summer heat.

Much of Vietnam is sub-tropical and hence there is an astonishing variety of fresh produce. In Dalat, Vietnam's honeymoon capital, terraced hills are so abundant with vegetables and fruits, that many residents are natural vegetarians and, with tea and coffee from surrounding plantations, Ho Chi Minh City is lavishly supplied with fresh daily produce. Lowlands extending from the South China Sea nurture grapes and joint-venture wineries are developing.

Vietnam's 3,260 kilometres of coastline yields gleaming fish and seafood. Fish are also caught in the Red, Perfume and Mekong Rivers, as well as in countless canals and ponds.

The People

Whether bent in the fields (80 per cent of people toil in agriculture), spinning silk, making lacquerware, copying famous artworks of European masters, manning stalls, endlessly serving food, hobbling along streets burdened by their *don ganh*, or working in offices, the Vietnamese are friendly and hospitable.

Vietnamese people don't demonstrate any resentment towards nationalities with whom they have previously been at war. But be prepared for amusing aggression from competing owners of *pho* shops seeking

PEOPLE

custom and from bargaining riders of cyclos (cycle-cabs for one or two) eager to take visitors anywhere.

A mix of Asian religions, Christianity and minority Islam, the Vietnamese people celebrate the seven-day *Tet* festival (Vietnamese New Year) with great gusto, eating special foods such as sticky rice, yellow beans and spiced pig fat boiled for six hours in banana leaves. Sweetmeats, dried, sugar and salted fruits are sold en masse. *Tet* occurs in the lunar calendar in late January or early February. Wandering Souls' Day on the 15th day of the seventh month is the second largest festival in Vietnam. Gifts, mainly fruits, are taken to pagodas and sweets to houses as tributes to the souls of forgotten dead.

Food is paramount in the Mid-Autumn festival on the 15th day of the eighth lunar month; a festival filled with bright, noisy, night processions. Other *tets* and a January rice-cooking festival, out of Hanoi, also liven the lunar calendar.

Vietnam is a bountiful paradise in poverty. Yet its proud people don't eat to live. They live to eat.

Daily food in
VIETNAM

Le Petit Dejeuner

Just before sunrise in Hanoi's old quarter, courting couples called it a day after conquering the night with their screaming motor cycles. Apart from crowding into Internet cafes or flirting over *pho*, motorcycles are the only cheap entertainment. Girls, some wearing *ao dai*, their national costume of long white pants, modest thigh-length, wrist-touching tops, coolie hats and gloves (to keep hands pale-skinned), were home (unaware that UNESCO hopes to classify the *ao dai* as a human heritage cultural object).

Street sweepers shuffled slowly. Light filtered through an avenue of leafy trees. An old woman painstakingly arranged eggs in the baskets of her *doh ganh*; white in one, brown in the other. Shopkeepers and residents emerged to peruse hawkers' vegetables, fruit, meat and fish. Flower vendors offered bright blooms from their the baskets of their bicycles. A soup seller's business was brisk with manicurists and pedicurists sitting on small plastic stools. Between glamorising working women, they spooned up *chao* (rice porridge) or soup, digging for noodles with chopsticks.

An aged street barber massaged the neck of his disabled son who sat in a primitive wheelchair. The barber was alternately cutting hair and sipping tea. The tea, I was told, is far too strong for females in the morning.

Daily food in
VIETNAM

A pre-World War II Citroen halted by a large pottery shop where salesgirls ate *pho* with salad. In French, a woman offered me sticky rice in banana-leaf parcels – just to taste, no charge unless I liked it. I'd had my *pho* fix. In plush hotels, French continental breakfast rolls, croissants and pastries were baking. In the fields, men were drinking tea together and eating rice with fish sauce.

Hanoi's seven million people began the day. Their repasts were on the move as they were everywhere in Vietnam. Baguette bikes tow mobile stalls until dark. Weeks later, in southern Dalat, I grabbed a morning, melt-in-mouth, hot, puff-pastry stuffed with pâté from a patisserie and became hooked.

In Dalat, inhabitants also eat *chao*, but it is quite unlike the bland rice porridge eaten elsewhere in Vietnam. Dalat *chao* is also favoured in the evening as fodder to fuel cooling bodies in mountainous terrain. This thick gruel is pork broth based, with meat or fish chunks, garlic and chilli oil added, and topped with coriander, bean sprouts and black pepper. It makes a filling dinner.

In the Mekong Delta's Cai Rang and on Phu Quoc, one of several islands (and Vietnam's most famous source of *nuoc cham*), floating marketeers feed dawn risers. Each fragile vessel carries a speciality – fruits, vegetables, fish, pork, rice, noodles, baguettes, tea, coffee and even breakfast beer.

Out of Ninh Binh town, my friend Jillian and I glided in a traditional rowboat through Tam Coc (meaning three caves) along the Ngo Dong River. (This river supplies a canal system for rice irrigation.) Spectacular rock formations were like those in Halong Bay and were reminiscent of China's Guilin and Yangzhou. Sole westerners, other than holidaying French people, we were assailed in French by boat folk. They'd row or pole back a long way to the port village for breakfast or lunch if they didn't have *pho*, fish, water, beer, fruit, plus embroidered napery, hats, film, even rice hooch. Such is the enthusiasm of boat vendors.

Jillian became addicted to Vietnamese smoothies – not the same as western thick-shakes. Melting ice is blended with sweetened condensed milk, a mint sprig, lime or lemon juice, plus any fruit or, for savoury smoothies, avocado, tomato, pumpkin, together or alone, garnished with coriander. Created for western budget-backpackers, smoothies have been happily adopted by busy, young Vietnamese as fruitful breakfast starters and as lunchtime coolers.

Some children breakfast at home but are more likely to eat market food with a parent before schools starts at 7.30 am. They have a choice of either morning or afternoon sessions. The second session begins after lunch at home or at the market.

Although coffee aficionados might disagree, Vietnamese coffee, brewed strong and slowly, is super. It is always consumed at breakfast and after dinner, with milk or cream and sugar. Tea is endemic to Vietnam and its serving is elevated to an art form as in China. Black tea is cheap. Green tea is expensive. In the central mountains, artichoke tea is popular.

Dejeuner - Ah, Lunch

Since first light, markets in cities, towns, villages and on fishing waterfronts are abuzz. While people eat all day, snacking on desserts rather than enjoying them as a meal finale. Those who can go home for lunch, do, but not many do, judging by the crammed street eateries, crowded cafes, restaurants and markets.

Westerners recognise much of the Vietnamese lunch fare as snack food or appetisers: spring rolls, cold or hot, and more tasty titbits, (some can be found in the Appetiser section of this book). On sale for lunch in Vietnam are noodles, rice cakes, baguettes, grilled meats, seafood, ubiquitous *pho* and plain steamed rice with fish sauce.

From 11 am to noon and onward, Vietnam lunches. At home, the women cook. Professional cooks and chefs are mostly men. The home menu will be rice with soup plus two to three other dishes, one a salad, or sautéed, fried or boiled vegetables. Non-working weekend lunches are leisurely for Vietnamese families who, if they can afford it, add an extra dish or two, usually on Sunday. Fish or meat is not always eaten daily because meat, particularly beef, is more expensive than vegetables, which are abundant. Sheep are not bred in Vietnam. Edible leaves garnish and wrap food in neat packets.

Be wary of salads in Vietnam. While frequently combined with meat, poultry or fish, the vegies may not have been washed in safe water. (But you can prepare the salads in this book in your own kitchen.) Monosodium glutamate is in many Vietnamese dishes. (It's allergenic for some people and has therefore been deleted from the authentic recipes to follow. See the glossary for other food substitutes.)

Utensils are simple: a pot for rice, one for slow cooking, an essential mortar and pestle, (in the west, a blender or food processor) and a couple of pans (a wok is unnecessary but helpful). Some Vietnamese use a coolie-hat shaped pan, similar to a wok. Add to this list, sharp large and small knives and an optional cleaver for do-it-yourself butchering, a chopping board, chopsticks, bowls with saucers, small bowls for sauces, serving dishes with spoons and tiny cups for tea.

Le Diner - Home at Last

Dinner is time for hard-working parents to be reunited with children and elderly relatives. Dinner dishes are similar to home-prepared lunches, centred around the rice bowl and all served simultaneously with soup. Dinner could comprise up to eight dishes on special occasions. Fruits are usually served for dessert.

Before eating, guests wait until the elder host is seated and until he or she places something in their bowl. That's in the north. Southerners are more casual. It is customary to leave a tasty leftover in a serving bowl to be offered to the host. He or she will then offer it back to the guest. Some morsels should remain in bowls to indicate the family has been generous. But do not leave rice. It is too precious to waste. A belief exists that if rice, the staple, is not eaten on earth, a departed soul could be denied basic sustenance in another world.

In the countryside, cooking is outdoors over a coal brazier. With no refrigeration, shopping at the market may be done twice daily. Small city kitchens may have only two gas or electric hotplates. Most don't have ovens and hence the method of slow pot-cooking. Other Vietnamese

cooking methods are sautéing, stir- and deep-frying, boiling and brazier grilling. Vietnamese use a garlic-infused oil — peanut oil heated with crushed garlic added after the oil, hot but not boiling, has been removed from the burner. Kept in a jar, garlic oil lasts about a week and is brushed on barbecued meat or fish, noodles, bread and vegetables. Decoration of Vietnamese dishes is important.

Drinks include fruit and sugarcane juices and soft fizzy drinks, similar to those in the West. Worth a try is (flat) bird's nest canned drink. Coconut milk is drunk through straws from punctured fresh coconuts. Few women drink alcohol. Men will imbibe light, refreshing beer with a meal out but most drinking is at home — and ice cools the beer! Wine, introduced by the French, is an acceptable accompaniment to Vietnamese food which is only as fiery as the diner dares and accompanied by *nuoc cham* or fresh, chopped chilli. Moonshine is made from fermented sticky rice, husks, water and yeast. It was once only the tipple of mountain ethnic minority people at celebrations but is now more popular in cities. It is cheap and readily available. Depending on where it is made and how long it is fermented, the intensity of Vietnamese moonshine varies from 'funny-bland-taste' to knockout 'POW'! (Use vodka as a substitute aperitif at home.) As in Korea and China, snake wine comes with the viper in the bottle. Wine is a misnomer in this instance. It's as spirited as strong rice rotgut, so beware. Tastes are similar.

Eating Out

In Vietnam, *pho* houses and markets are must-sees. Markets can be smelly but glorious flower perfumes are overwhelming. You can eat confidently from street vendors if selections are hot. Bamboo sections or pieces of metal being banged together will be a noodle-knocker's signal that noodles in soup (and occasionally grilled meat, seafood or spring rolls) are nearby. You'll eat cheaply and well in- or in-front-of a simple shop. There will be no menu. Just point.

Similar eating establishments are called *com* (meaning rice). These are family-run, no-frills places. Some display picture menus if the *com* is a shop. Otherwise, eat in the street — perfect for people-watching.

Eager to try Hue's legendary seafood-stuffed crêpes (recipe included in this book), I wandered into a com There was no menu but the place had indoor and street seating. The intelligent old father was deaf and dumb. I drew a primitive picture. He rushed to the miniscule back yard to his wife and daughter and returned with a selection of canned drinks in his hands. I chose light beer. Soon, I was served by the women who awaited my appraisal. 'Magnifique' I attested honestly. (Some acquaintance with French language is handy in Vietnam.)

Dog, cat, snake, field mice and rats, and embryo ducks from eggs are served in certain restaurants (recipes not included in these pages). Legs of frogs are fine, the French have said for a long time, and snails too. Do try eel the eel recipe in this book.

A che is a shop or stall selling desserts, cakes and sweetmeats. Pancake outlets serve savoury to sweet pancakes but differ from western pancake parlours. Street waterfront restaurants abound in river and sea ports, indoors and out. Upmarket establishments are found in major Vietnamese cities. Waiters may not speak English but a translated menu will signify the number of the dish. Vietnamese music or European classical, mainly French composers, provide a soothing background. In international hotels, ambience will be a la France — neatly laid tables, good service and Vietnamese/French/English menus. If unaffordable for dining, go to a legendary hotel like the Rex in Saigon for a drink, a rooftop view or elegant environment. More and more Grand French mansions are being restored into high-class restaurants.

In Vietnam, offer flowers as gifts to hosts. For Mai, Tet, Hanh and Madame Thu, I chose big bouquets. Their ribbons streaked towards the sky in peak traffic as we whirled four-vehicles-wide on my last suicidal cycle ride.

'Love our country,' they cried. I do. Even if you never visit Vietnam, I hope you can imagine a scenically sensational country and its struggling, warm, people through a delicate yet hearty cuisine boasting more than 5,000 dishes. Hue's 19th century emperor Tu Duc demanded 50 dishes in each single meal, never to be served more than twice in the same year. Imperial chefs created more than 2,000 dishes during his reign. Aghast? Envious? The portions were tiny.

Kerry Kenihan

appetisers

Roll on a
WRAP

'It's a wrap,' says a film director when a movie scene is finally finished to satisfaction. 'It's a wrap' in a Vietnamese kitchen, street market and or hawker stall means a super snack. At home, it signifies the scene has just been set for the beginning of a meal or party – cocktail, luncheon or dinner – and a wrap is appropriate as so many Vietnamese appetisers are tasty parcels.

Wraps may be deep- or shallow-fried, steamed or packed in fresh edible leaves – banana, lettuce, spinach, or cabbage – to be served cool. Wraps are delectable dollops of mixed ingredients in rice paper, crepes, thicker pancakes, omelettes, squid or even snails.

Spring rolls come with nuoc cham (fish sauce for dipping, as distinct from bottled fish sauce. As China has exerted great influence on Vietnamese food, its soy sauce is often an ingredient in wraps too. Soy sauce is likely to be on Vietnamese tables as a dipping sauce too and many westerners prefer it to fish sauce. Use Vietnamese, Thai, Japanese or Chinese soy sauce. American-made is too salty. Finely ringed, small, seeded, red chilli is also a separate, spring roll accompaniment.

Sensational stuffed crêpes and seafood threaded on sugar cane were both created in the ancient imperial court of Hue and are Vietnamese specialties, particularly in Central and South Vietnam.

WHITE SAUCE

Ingredients
45g/1½oz butter
3 tablespoons plain flour
200mL/7fl oz full-fat milk
salt and black pepper

Method
1. Heat the butter in a saucepan, then fry the shallots for 5 minutes. Stir in the flour and cook for 2 minutes, stirring. Stir in the milk and cook for 20 minutes stirring often.

HUE STUFFED PANCAKE

Ingredients
oil for frying
55g/2oz seasoned flour
2 eggs, beaten
extra oil for deep frying

Batter:
85g/3oz rice flour
½ cup coconut milk
3 eggs, beaten
pinch salt

Filling:
½ tablespoon peeled, chopped ginger
1 clove garlic, chopped
1 tablespoon soy sauce
½ cup/125mL/4½fl oz white sauce (see below left)
145g/5oz crab meat
85g/3oz mushrooms, chopped
30g/1oz spring onions, chopped
30g/1oz bean sprouts
salt and pepper

To Serve:
lettuce leaves
chopped coriander
nuoc cham
1 red chilli, seeded and finely sliced

Method
1. Combine rice flour, coconut milk, eggs and salt to make a batter. Heat some oil in a 20cm/8in pan (preferably non-stick) add enough batter to coat base. Cook for 2 minutes. Repeat with remaining batter.

2. Blend ginger, garlic, soy and white sauce. Add crab meat, mushrooms, spring onions, and bean sprouts and season to taste. Place a spoonful of the mixture on to each pancake. Tuck in ends and roll up so mixture doesn't escape.

3. Carefully roll each pancake in seasoned flour then in beaten egg. Deep-fry until golden. Serve on lettuce leaves, sprinkled with chopped coriander, accompanied by nuoc cham.

Note: For variation, use thinly rolled puff pastry instead of pancakes. Pancakes can also be filled and served without deep frying.

Serves 8

PRAWN CRÊPES

Ingredients

255g/9oz rice flour
1 teaspoon salt
1½ teaspoons sugar
1 cup/250mL/8¾fl oz coconut milk (canned)
1 cup/250mL/8¾fl oz water
½ teaspoon ground turmeric
200g/7oz shelled king prawns
200g/7oz bean shoots
100g/3½ oz pork fillet or chicken
1 onion, sliced
peanut oil (for frying)
nuoc cham

To Garnish:
Vietnamese mint leaves
lettuce leaves

Method

1. Mix together rice flour, salt, sugar, coconut milk, water and turmeric until the batter is smooth.

2. Wash and dry prawns and chop roughly. Wash bean shoots and set aside.

3. Dice the pork or chicken.

4. Heat a large frying pan and pour in a little oil. Add pork, onion and prawns, and cook, stirring constantly, until prawns change colour and pork is cooked through.

5. Pour enough batter over mixture to cover ingredients, top with some bean shoots and cover pan with a lid. Cook for 2 minutes until crisp. Turn over and cook the other side until golden.

To serve: Place a Vietnamese mint leaf on a piece of the crêpe. Enclose in a lettuce leaf and drizzle nuoc cham over. Eat immediately.

Serves 4

NUOC CHAM DIPPING SAUCE

Ingredients

125g/4½oz or golden caster sugar
1 cup hot water
½ cup Vietnamese fish sauce
1 tablespoon white rice vinegar
75mL/2½floz lime juice
2–4 small red or green chillies, finely chopped
3–5 large garlic cloves, finely chopped

Method

1. Put the sugar in a bowl and pour the hot water over it, stirring until it is completely dissloved. Add all the other ingredients, stir well and allow to cool to room temperature.

2. This dipping sauce can be kept in an airtight container in the refrigerator for up to 7 days.

MADAME THU'S STEAMED EGG ROLL

Ingredients

2 duck eggs

15g/½oz dried wood-ear mushrooms

rice wine or dry sherry

oil or pork fat for frying

2 cups water

1 banana leaf or muslin

200g/7oz pork mince

1 teaspoon sesame seeds

2 cloves garlic, minced

2 finely chopped pimentos
   or seeded red chillis

2 dessertspoons sugar

2 dessertspoons fish sauce

pinch black pepper

15g/½oz field mushrooms

1 piece hot spicy cooked sausage,
   about 17½cm /7in

length of string

nuoc cham

To Garnish:

slices of cucumber, tomatoes,
parboiled cauliflower florets
and fresh parsley sprigs

Method

1. Soak dried mushrooms in hot water for about 30 minutes until soft. Meanwhile, separate eggs into 2 bowls; whites in one, yolks in the other. Beat both, adding a little wine to the whites to reduce the eggy odor and a little to the yolks make a medium thick consistency.

2. Season a pan with a little pork fat or oil, add some pork to flavour pan. Stir-fry over medium heat, then remove. Add egg white mixture to pan and, when firm, remove in pancake form and place on a plate. Re-season pan with more pork fat or oil, then pour off excess oil and add beaten yolk and wine mixture.

3. Lower heat. When bubbles form on top of egg, turn off heat and place omelette on another plate. Boil 2 cups water, slip banana leaf in to clean and soften. Strain and place leaf or moistened muslin on a board.

4. Mix pork with sesame seeds, garlic, pimento or chilli, sugar, fish sauce and pepper to taste. Remove stalks from dried mushrooms and discard. Add fresh mushrooms and pound until thin. Heat quickly in pan. Remove.

5. Place yolk omlette on a board. Spread one quarter raw pork mix over a spatula. Top with mushrooms. Add another layer each of pork and mushrooms, place egg white circle on top then add another pork layer. Carefully press with oiled rolling pin, add single sausage and trim. Gently roll and fill in roll end with pork.

6. Place roll on banana leaf or muslin, tuck in ends and bind with string to hold shape. Steam in a double boiler for about 17 minutes. Remove and cool then refrigerate until cold.

7. Arrange half-moon shapes of cucumber around the edge of a serving plate then, inside the cricle, of cucumber arrange tomato slices, a heart shape. Remove leaf or muslin from cold roll, slice in 1cm/1in thickness and arrange in middle of the plate. Top with parsley sprigs.

Note: These hor d'oeuvres are intended for a Valentine's Day party. Serve with nuoc cham.

Makes 6 to 7 pieces

SPRING ROLLS

Ingredients

20g/²/₃oz vermicelli (green bean thread)

3 tablespoons vegetable oil

3 cloves garlic, finely chopped

310g/11oz minced chicken
    (or half crab meat, half pork)

¹/₄ cabbage, cut into fine strips

1 carrot, cut into thin strips

2 spring onions, finely chopped

¹/₂ teaspoon salt

1 teaspoon sugar

¹/₂ teaspoon white pepper

1 tablespoon oyster sauce

20–25 rice-paper wrappers (see page 16)

1 egg, beaten

extra oil for deep frying

nuoc cham (see page 13)

To Garnish:

lettuce and mint leaves

Method

1. Soak vermicelli for 5 minutes in hot water until soft. Drain, cut into 5cm/2in lengths and reserve.

2. Heat 3 tablespoons oil in wok or pan. Add garlic and chicken (or crab and pork) and cook about 8 minutes, separating so ingredients don't adhere to pan. Add cabbage, carrot, spring onions and vermicelli and cook on high heat for 3 minutes or until vegetables soften.

3. Turn off heat, add salt, sugar, pepper and oyster sauce. Stir to mix well. When mixture is cool, brush each side of the rice wrappers with water or they will dry and break. Place 1 tablespoon of the mixture into each wrapper, turn sides in first, roll and seal each with beaten egg. Refrigerate until needed.

4. Heat extra oil in wok or pan. Deep-fry rolls until golden. Serve on lettuce leaves garnished with lettuce and mint and serve with bottled sweet chilli sauce or nuoc cham.

Makes 20

RICE PAPER WRAPPERS

Ingredients

85g/3oz rice flour

3 cups water

salt to taste

oil

Method

1. Make batter with flour, water and salt. Three-quarter fill the base of a double boiler with water and stretch a piece of muslin or cheesecloth firmly over the boiler's top and bind securely with string.

2. Bring water to boil. Brush fabric with oil and pour a little batter on, using a swirling motion with a spoon to spread it into a circle. Cover with a lid and leave a minute or so until firmed. Carefully lift the wrapper with a spatula and set aside. Repeat until all batter is used. Wrappers can be stuffed with pre-cooked filling and served cold or filled and deep fried.

Note: After making rice paper wrappers or opening a bought packet, dip the wrappers in water to soften and cover with a damp tea towel to retain moisture.

Makes about 20

VIETNAMESE HERB SALAD ROLLS WITH HOME-MADE PEANUT SAUCE (opposite)

Ingredients

55g/2oz packet cellophane noodles

3 tablespoons rice vinegar

1 tablespoon fish sauce

4 tablespoons roasted peanuts, crushed

12 large prawns, cooked and finely chopped

20 Thai basil leaves, finely sliced

10 Asian mint leaves, finely sliced

$1/4$ cup fresh coriander, finely chopped

4 leaves of Chinese cabbage (bok choy)

2 cabbage leaves, finely shredded

5 spring onions, julienned

1 medium carrot, finely shredded

12–16 rice paper wrappers (20cm/8in)

Peanut Sauce:

2 tablespoons peanut oil

5 cloves garlic, minced

$1/2$ small red chilli, minced

5 tablespoons peanut butter

$1 1/2$ tablespoons tomato paste

3 tablespoons hoi sin sauce

1 teaspoon sugar

1 teaspoon fish sauce

$3/4$ cup water

$1/4$ cup peanuts (crushed)

Method

1. Soak the cellophane noodles in a bowl full of hot water to cover for 5–10 minutes or until tender. Drain immediately and rinse with cold water (to halt the cooking time). Cut noodles, with scissors, to a manageable length and toss with vinegar, fish sauce, crushed peanuts and prawns.

2. In a large bowl, mix together herbs, cabbage leaves (both sorts), spring onions, noodle mixture and grated carrot and toss thoroughly.

3. Working with 1 wrapper at a time, soak rice wrapper in warm water for 30 seconds and lie it on a flat surface. On each wrapper, place a small quantity of the mixed vegetable/noodle filling. Roll up tightly, folding the sides in, to enclose the filling. Continue rolling and folding until all ingredients are used.

4. To make peanut sauce, heat oil and sauté garlic and minced chilli until softened (about 2 minutes), then add all remaining ingredients and whisk over moderate heat. Bring to the boil and simmer until thickened slightly (about 3 minutes).

5. To serve, slice each roll on the diagonal, then rest one half over the other. Serve the sauce separately in a small pot for dipping.

Note: As these wrappers do fry successfully, you may like to serve half of them fresh and half of them fried.

Makes 20

herb salad rolls

SHRIMP BALLS

Ingredients

3 drops rice wine or dry sherry

salt and black pepper, to taste

1 teaspoon sugar

55g/2oz pork fat, minced

225g/8oz shrimp or shelled prawns

1 dessertspoon finely ground peppercorns

1 small brown onion, finely chopped

225g/8oz minced pork

1 dessertspoon freshly chopped dill or parsley

1 chicken stock cube

1 egg, beaten

handful breadcrumbs

vegetable oil for frying and handling

1 small red chilli, seeded
    and finely chopped (optional)

To Garnish:

lettuce leaves, fresh coriander leaves
and peeled carrot strips

Method

1. Combine drops of wine, pork fat, black pepper, sugar and a little salt in a bowl. Sit bowl in another bowl of hot water to melt the fat. (The Vietnamese would the bowl into the sun to warm and melt until the fat is transparent.)

2. Chop shrimps or prawns very finely until mushy. Place in bowl. Add peppercorns and a little extra salt and pepper.

3. Fry onion until transparent, drain oil and add onion to pork mince. Combine, add shrimps and dill or parsley and/or optional chilli with shrimps and pork fat.

4. Crush stock cube finely and mix with breadcrumbs. Work some oil into your hands, form walnut-sized balls and dip each ball in beaten egg and breadcrumbs mix. Deep-fry in oil in a wok or pan until golden. Quickly drain on kitchen paper and serve on a plate layered with lettuce. Top with coriander leaves and strips of finely peeled carrot.

Makes 12–14 balls

SEAFOOD SUGAR CANE SKEWERS

Ingredients

1½ cups shrimps, or prawn or crab meat, minced

black pepper to taste

1 clove garlic, crushed

½ teaspoon fish sauce

1½ teaspoons sugar

1½ tablespoons vegetable oil

8 sticks sugar cane, 10cm/4in long

To Garnish:

1 red chilli, seeded and finely sliced

1 lime, sliced into 8 wedges

mint

coriander and lettuce leaves

1 cup sweet and sour sauce
   (see page 39)

Method

1. Add pepper, garlic, fish sauce and sugar to seafood. Pound or blend until combined and refrigerate, covered, for hours.

2. Oil your hands, divide seafood paste into 8 and mould each portion smoothly around the centre of each sugar cane skewer.

3. Grill or barbecue over medium heat until golden and crisp or bake in a moderate oven for 15–20 minutes. Place on serving plates with lettuce, mint, coriander leaves, slices of chilli and lime slices attractively arranged. Serve with sweet and sour sauce.

Makes 8

PRAWNS IN CARAMEL

Ingredients

455g/1 lb raw prawns

5 spring onions

4¹/₂ tablespoons sugar

7 tablespoons water

oil for frying

4 cloves garlic, finely chopped

1 tablespoon fish sauce

1 tablespoon lime or lemon juice

pinch salt

1 tablespoon brown sugar

¹/₃ green capsicum, to garnish

Method

1. Shell, and devein prawns. Remove heads but retain tails. Finely chop 3 spring onions. Cut the remaining 2 into thin strips 2¹/₂cm/1in long.

2. In a saucepan, heat sugar until golden, add 3 tablespoons of water and stir until sugar dissolves. Boil then simmer gently for about 3 minutes until caramel darkens but doesn't burn. Remove pot from heat and add remaining water. Take care caramel does not spatter. Reheat, stirring quickly, to remove lumps.

3. Heat oil in heavy pan and fry chopped spring onion and garlic over medium heat. Add prawns for a few minutes until prawns are pink. Slowly pour fish sauce and warm caramel over prawn mixture. Combine and cook 1 minute before adding lime or lemon juice, salt, brown sugar and spring onion slivers. Stir together and serve topped with capsicum strips.

Serves 4

soups

Pho GOODNESS SAKE

On a short or extended stay in Vietnam, a visitor could exist totally on soup - and yet never become bored nor fail to be tantalised.

When Lewis Carroll's Mock Turtle extolled the delights of beautiful soup of the evening to the Gryphon and Alice in Wonderland, he had obviously never heard of Vietnam where soup begins, sustains and ends each day. *Pho* (pronounced 'fur') is the addictive national dish based on a rich, slowly cooked, clear, beef consumme with noodles, aromatic with spices, ginger and cinnamon essential. *Pho* is secretively prepared to family recipes by competitive sellers. Their extra ingredients give *pho* subtle variety. Gourmets and food writers have described pho as Vietnam in a bowl of soul comfort. It derives from the French *pot au feu*.

Light, as consomme, but chock full of vegetables, meat or fish, with Chinese, Thai and French influences, Vietnamese soups make marvellously hearty lunches when served with crusty bread and, perhaps, a tossed green salad.

Sour fish soup is almost as much an institution as beef *pho*. Fish and/or seafood in soup always presents as a class act. To really show off, prepare a favourite Tet, (New Year(festival first course cabbage parcels in soup. crab & asparagus soup features on many Vietnamese menus.

For fun at brunch, introduce *chao* or rice porridge to friends. It can comprise chicken, duck, fish or oysters combined with pork and at least one green vegetable. You can experiment as the Vietnamese do. Sliced red chilli, fish sauce and black pepper should be served in separate, small, shared bowls for diners to add to their *chao* at liberty.

Soups can be served in individual bowls or a large tureen for self-service at table. Supply guests with chopsticks as well as soup spoons.

FISH WITH TOMATO AND DILL

Ingredients
3 medium tomatoes
750g/1 1/2 lb freshwater fish fillets
6 cups chicken stock
2 tablespoons chopped fresh dill
salt and pepper
extra fresh dill

Method
1. Chop tomatoes into wedges. Cut fish into large bite-sized chunks. Boil stock. Add fish, and turn down to simmer for 6 minutes. Skim surface froth and add tomatoes, dried dill and salt and pepper to taste.

2. Simmer a little longer until fish is cooked but not breaking up. Serve in large bowl or individual bowls and garnish with fresh dill.

Note: This is a chunky soup is a good starter or part of a multi-coursed Vietnamese meal. It also makes a family lunch or dinner served with fresh baguettes and a salad.

Serves 6

BEEF PHO

Ingredients

225g/8oz thick steak in one piece

rice noodles

455g/1 lb flat, thick, dried noodles

2 tablespoons fish sauce

1/2 cup of bean sprouts

1 brown onion, thinly sliced

3 spring onions, finely chopped

1/2 cup fresh coriander, torn into sprigs

1/2 cup vietnamese mint leaves, chopped

1 small red chilli, seeded and sliced into rings

2 limes cut into wedges

Stock:

12 cups water

1kg/2 1/4lb shin beef bones

340g/12oz gravy beef

1 large brown, unpeeled onion, halved

3 medium pieces unpeeled ginger, sliced

pinch of salt

1 cinnamon stick

6 whole cloves

6 peppercorns

6 coriander seeds

4 whole star anise

2 unpeeled carrots, cut into chunks

Method

1. To make stock, pour water into a large pot and add shin bones and gravy beef, bring to the boil. Skim off foaming scum from surface. Turn heat to medium-low, partly cover and simmer for 2 hours, skimming often. Add remaining stock ingredients. Simmer another 90 minutes and remove from heat.

2. Drain through a fine sieve , reserving stock. Discard bones, carrots, onion and spices. When cool, skim fat from stock. Cut gravy beef finely across the grain. Slice steak to paper thinn slices and set aside.

3. Soak rice noodles in warm water for about 20 minutes until soft. Drain and set aside.

4. Return stock pot to boil with fish sauce then reduce heat to very low. Fill a separate large pot three-quarters full of water and bring to the boil. Add dried noodles and washed bean sprouts. Continue boiling until noodles are tender but not mushy. Bean sprouts should retain some crispness.

5. Pour boiling stock into 6 serving bowls, add drained noodles then top equally with shin meat, raw onion rings, chopped spring onions, and raw steak slices, and garnish with coriander and mint leaves.

Note: Diners may help themselves to chilli rings and lime wedges. This recipe is also good with to chicken which takes less time to cook.

Serves 6

ASPARAGUS AND CRAB MEAT SOUP (MANG TAY NAU CUA)

Ingredients

4 cups chicken broth

1 tablespoon plus 2 teaspoons fish sauce

$1/2$ teaspoon sugar

$1/4$ teaspoon salt

1 tablespoon vegetable oil

6 shallots, chopped

2 cloves garlic, chopped

225g/8oz crab meat

freshly ground black pepper

2 tablespoons corn flour or arrowroot,
   mixed with 2 tablespoons cold water

1 egg, lightly beaten

425g/15oz white asparagus spears, cut into
   $2^{1}/2$cm/1in sections, reserves canning liquid

1 tablespoon shredded coriander

1 spring onion, thinly sliced

Method

1. Combine broth, 1 tablespoon of fish sauce, sugar and salt in a $3^{1}/2$ litre/3 quart soup pot. Bring to the boil. Reduce the heat and simmer.

2. Meanwhile, heat oil in a skillet. Add shallots and garlic and stir-fry until aromatic. Add crab meat, the remaining 2 teaspoons of fish sauce and black pepper to taste.

3. Stir-fry over high heat for 1 minute. Set aside.

4. Bring the soup to a boil. Add corn flour mixture and stir gently until the soup thickens and is clear. While the soup is actively boiling, add egg and stir gently.

5. Continue to stir for about 1 minute. Add crab meat mixture and asparagus with its canning liquid. Cook gently until heated through.

6. Transfer the soup to a heated tureen. Sprinkle on the coriander, spring onion and freshly ground black pepper.

Note: If white asparagus is unavailable, use frozen or fresh asparagus to the broth from the very beginning and cook until tender, before adding the remaining ingredients).

Serves 4–6

HOT AND SOUR FISH SOUP

Ingredients

1kg/35oz firm-fleshed fish such as red snapper,
1 1/2 tablespoons nuoc cham (see page 13)
1/4 teaspoon white pepper
1 spring onion, chopped
6 cups water
2 stalks lemongrass, cut into 5cm/2in lengths
   and crushed lightly
55g/2oz tamarind pulp
3/4 cup boiling water
1 tablespoon sugar
3/4 cup sliced bamboo shoots
1 cup sliced pineapple
2 tomatoes, cut into wedges
1 cup beans prouts
mixed Vietnamese herbs such as coriander,
   bitter herb, Asian basil
deep fried to shallots
lime wedges
sliced chilli

Method

1. Remove head, fins and tail from fish and cut
   into 8–10 large pieces. Combine fish, fish
   sauce, pepper and spring onion, allow to
   marinate for 15 minutes.

2. Place water in a large saucepan and bring to
   the boil. Add the fish with its juices and
   lemongrass. Reduce heat and simmer for
   20 minutes.

3. Meanwhile, combine tamarind pulp and
   boiling water and allow to soak for
   15 minutes. Strain mixture through
   a fine sieve and discard pulp.

4. Add the tamarind liquid, sugar, bamboo
   shoots, pineapple and tomatoes to the pan.
   Simmer for 4–5 minutes until fish is tender.

5. Divide bean sprouts amongst serving bowls
   and spoon hot soup over. Sprinkle with
   fresh herbs and deep-fried shallots Serve
   with lime wedges and sliced chilli on the
   side.

Serves 4–6

CABBAGE PARCELS IN SOUP

Ingredients

24 cabbage leaves

6 spring onions

4 tablespoons coriander, finely chopped

1 cup pork, minced

1/2 cup prawns, minced

6 1/4 cups chicken or pork stock

2 1/2 tablespoons fish sauce

Method

1. Blanch cabbage leaves in boiling water and cut away any tough sections from their bases.

2. Cut white ends from spring onions and finely chop 4 white heads. Slice 2 for garnish. Halve, lengthwise green stalks, into strips.

3. Mix well chopped spring onions and 2 tablespooons of coriander with pork and prawns. Season with pepper.

4. Into each cabbage leaf, place 1 tablespoon of mixture. Fold the leaf base over then the outer edges and roll up. Carefully tie up each roll with a length of green spring onion and place parcels gently into boiling stock to cook for 6 minutes.

5. Lift parcels into bowls, pour a cup of stock over each and garnish with remaining sliced spring onions and coriander. Dip rolls into fish sauce when eating.

Serves 6

DUCK AND NUT SOUP

Ingredients

6 pieces duck or chicken

peanut oil

8 cups water or stock

2 teaspoons salt

2 cups mixed nuts, crushed

¹/₂ can of lychees or loganberries, drained

To Garnish:

fresh coriander

Method

1. Cut duck into bite-sized pieces. Fry in a little peanut oil until golden. Boil stock or water with salt. Add duck and simmer for 45 minutes. Skim till broth is clear.

2. Add nuts and simmer another 45 minutes. Add lychees or loganberries 5 minutes before serving. Garnish with coriander leaves.

Serves 6

VERMICELLI AND CHICKEN SOUP

Ingredients

1 cup chicken breast chunks

225g/8oz Chinese mung bean vermicelli

$^1\!/_2$ cup of dried wood ear mushrooms, soaked
   (or $^1\!/_2$ cup canned button mushrooms, sliced)

salt to taste

$^1\!/_2$ teaspoon black or white pepper

2 tablespoons spring onions, chopped

Stock:

8 cups water

3 teaspoons fish sauce

1 onion, quartered

1$^1\!/_2$kg/3$^1\!/_3$ lb pork bones

455g/1 lb chicken wings, bones
   and/or leftover meat scraps

455g/1 lb of 2 of the following: whole carrot,
   quartered cauliflower, whole green beans
   and/or quarter of a cabbage

Method

1. Use packaged stock or make stock by boiling all ingredients together then simmering for 1 hour. Strain reduced stock and discard the bones and vegetables.

2. Boil chicken chunks in stock for 15 minutes, skimming scum from the surface. Add vermicelli and softened dried, mushrooms, removed stalks or canned mushrooms and cook until vermicelli is done.

3. Serve, season with salt and pepper and sprinkle with chopped spring onion.

Serves 6

meat

EAST

WEST

It's amazing that *pho* (beef soup) sellers ladle out their addictive national dish 24 hours a day without cutting costs considering meat and certainly beef, is relatively expensive in Vietnam. Family members often work in shifts to maintain the supply.

Home cooks utilise beef in many ways, usually in dishes loaded with other ingredients so that quantities can be kept smaller but the flavours enjoyed. The favourite meat is pork, bred prolifically, cheaper than beef and therefore able to be served more generously. Minced, pork often combines with seafood to give extra texture and taste to an appetiser or main dish. So, for extra recipes including pork, check the appetiser and seafood sections of this book. All meats combine magically with fish sauce – a constant essential in almost everything.

Vietnam's climate and terrain are unsuitable for the raising of sheep, so lamb and mutton are not included in authentic menus but can be prepared in place of beef and maybe pork in a western kitchen. Goats roam villages and around humble countryside dwellings but their meat doesn't make frequent appearances in Vietnamese restaurants or at street stalls.

In Vietnam, buffalo, frog, horse, rabbit, veal and venison are also eaten. Choose cheap cuts of beef for slow pot cooking and do try pork in caramel. It's a southern specialty. Meat, as well as chicken liver, is often used to make Vietnamese pâté, which can present as a luncheon dish with salad and baguette. Meat in parcel wrappers or skewered for barbecues is very popular.

Some recipes in this section call for garnish. All are planned to be part of a multi-coursed meal but for simple, family enjoyment, serve one course with rice or noodles and a salad or vegetables.

COCONUT PORK STEW

Ingredients

1 kg/35oz boneless pork, cut into large cubes
4 tablespoons vegetable oil
$2^{1}/_{2}$ cups coconut milk
6 hard-boiled eggs
3 spring onions
$^{1}/_{2}$ cup bean sprouts
nuoc cham (see page 13)

Marinade:

3 cloves garlic, crushed
pinch salt
$1^{1}/_{2}$ tablespoons sugar
4 tablespoons fish sauce

Method:

1. Combine marinade ingredients and add pork stirring so pork is completely covered. Marinate for at least 2 hours.

2. Heat oil in a heavy-based pan and add pork cubes, turning to sear all sides. Drain off any oil, add coconut milk and bring almost to the boil. Reduce heat, skim off surface scum and simmer, covered for about 45 minutes, until tender.

3. Peel hard-boiled eggs, add to pan and cook for about 10 minutes. Serve with nuoc cham and garnished with 3 spring onions cut into narrow 5cm/2in strips and $^{1}/_{2}$ cup of bean sprouts.

BEEF CURRY

Ingredients

1kg/35oz stewing beef, cubed

1 large onion, sliced

4 cloves garlic, crushed

2 tablespoons ginger, crushed

2 red chillis, seeded and chopped finely

3½ tablespoons hot curry powder

2 teaspoons turmeric

1 teaspoon black ground pepper

1 cup water

1½ teaspoons salt

4½ tablespoons fish sauce

⅓ cup vegetable oil

1 tablespoons sugar

3 large carrots, chopped

3 tablespoons cornflour

2¼ cups coconut milk

To Garnish:
coriander

Method

1. Combine beef, onion, garlic, ginger, chillis, curry powder, turmeric, pepper and 1 teaspoon of salt. Cover with plastic wrap and marinate in refriderator overnight. Turn occasionally.

2. Heat oil in a large, heavy-based saucepan, on high heat. Add beef, turning to seal in flavours before pouring in the water, ½ teaspoon salt and fish sauce. After boiling, cover with lid and turn down heat to simmer for about 1 hour until meat is cooked. Add sugar and carrots until they are done (about 15 minutes.)

3. Add cornflour to coconut milk, stirring to dissolve, and pour into curry, stirring for 10–15 minutes until curry thickens. Serve in a casserole with rice and salad. Garnish with coriander leaves.

Serves 4

CARAMELISED PORK

Ingredients

oil for frying
750g/1½lbs pork, cubed
2 cloves garlic, finely chopped
2 medium onions, sliced
⅓ cup/85g/3oz sugar
¾ cup water
1½ tablespoon fish sauce
1½ tablespoons lime juice
1 seeded red chilli, sliced and minced
½ teaspoon five spice powder
2 spring onions, chopped, for garnish

Method

1. Heat oil in a heavy-based pan, add pork cubes and turn until brown. Add garlic and onion and cook, stirring to separate onion rings until transparent. Remove from heat.

2. In a separate saucepan, mix sugar with water and stir over low heat until sugar dissolves. Bring to the boil then turn down to simmer, still stirring, until liquid is golden. Take pot off heat and carefully add fish sauce and lime juice. Return to heat, stirring quickly to remove any lumps, until the sauce reduces a little.

3. Quickly return pork, garlic and onions to reheat, add chilli and five spice and then caramel. Cook for 1 minute, stirring until combined. Transfer to serving dish and sprinkle spring onions on top.

Note: For easier washing up, pour boiling water immediately into pot in which caramel has cooked.

Serves 4

SIZZLING SPARE RIBS

Ingredients

8 dried mushrooms
2 spring onions
1 green capsicum
1 red chilli
500g/1 lb pork or beef spare ribs
oil for frying
$^1/_2$ teaspoon salt
$^1/_2$ teaspoon sugar
1 teaspoon dark soy sauce
$^1/_3$ cup water

Marinade:

$^1/_2$ teaspoon salt
$^1/_2$ teaspoon dry sherry
1 tablespoon light soy sauce
2 teaspoons cornflour

Sauce:

$^1/_2$ teaspoon cornflour
dash of sesame oil
ground black pepper
1$^1/_2$ tablespoons fish sauce

To Garnish:

mint sprigs

Method

1. Soak mushrooms 40 minutes in hot water. Remove stalks and discard. Cut spring onions into 3.5cm/1$^1/_2$ in pieces. Seed green pepper and chilli and cut into pieces. Combine marinade ingredients.

2. Cut spare ribs into large bite-sized pieces and marinate 30 minutes. Deep-fry until brown. Remove from heat. Sauté spring onions and mushrooms in oil, return ribs with $^1/_2$ teaspoon salt, sugar, dark soy sauce and $^1/_3$ cup water and stir-fry. Add capsicum, chilli and combined sauce ingredients.

3. Stir-fry, stirring, until capsicum just starts to lose crispness. Serve on a pre-heated heavy-metal grill pan so meat sizzles. Serve garnished with mint sprigs.

VIETNAMESE BEEF (opposite)

Ingredients

500g/1 lb fillet steak
1/2 cup vegetable oil
1 cup spring onions, sliced
500g/1 lb canned bamboo shoots,
    drained and sliced
pinch salt
1 1/2 tablespoons fish sauce
2 cloves garlic, minced
1/4 cup sesame seeds

Method

1. Slice steak into thin 5cm/2in strips. In a pan, heat half the oil and stir-fry beef for 1 minute then remove from pan.

2. Heat remaining oil and sauté spring onions and bamboo shoots for 3 minutes. Add salt and fish sauce and cook, stirring, for 5 minutes. Add garlic and cook for a further 2 minutes.

3. Return steak to pan and cook until just tender. Remove from heat, add sesame seeds, stir through and serve

Serves 4

BEEF WITH EGGPLANT

Ingredients

500g/1 lb eggplant, halved lengthwise
3 cloves garlic
vegetable oil
225g/8oz minced beef
2 tablespoons fish sauce
salt
freshly ground black pepper

Method

1. Chargrill eggplants over a barbecue or under a grill until skin blackens. Cool, peel and cut into pieces. Peel and mince garlic.

2. In a heavy-based pan, heat oil, then add garlic, stirring until soft. Add beef and cook, separating it with a spoon until beef loses its pinkness. Add eggplant, fish sauce and salt and pepper to taste. Turn down heat to simmer. before covering. Cook and cover about 25 minutes or until eggplant has lost its firmness.

Serves 4

BARBECUED PORK BALLS

Ingredients

1 tablespoon dry sherry
1 teaspoon salt
1 teaspoon sugar
3 cloves garlic, minced
500g/1 lb pork, finely minced
1 1/2 tablespoons ground rice
1 tablespoon fish sauce
1 1/2 tablespoons peanut oil

Method

1. Combine sherry, salt, sugar and garlic. Add pork, combine and let stand for 2 hours.

2. Add ground rice, fish sauce and peanut oil, mix well then form mixture into small balls, about walnut size. Put balls on to pre-soaked skewers, squeezing tightly so balls adhere to skewers.

3. Barbecue or grill, turning often, until pork is cooked.

Serves 4

BEEF, CAULIFLOWER AND MUSHROOM STIR-FRY (opposite)

Ingredients

225g/8oz steak, sliced into 5cm/2in strips
1/4 cauliflower, divided into florets
1/2 cup water or stock
1 1/2 teaspoons cornflour
2 tablespoons fish sauce
1 teaspoon oyster sauce
1 medium onion, cut lengthwise into 8 pieces
ground black pepper
vegetable oil
3 cloves garlic, finely chopped
200g/7oz fresh whole button mushrooms,
   reserving 1/2 cup canned liquid

To Garnish:
coriander sprigs

Method

1. Cut cauliflower florets in half. Mix water and mushroom liquid with cornflour, 1 tablespoon fish sauce and oyster sauce.

2. Pour 1 tablespoon of fish sauce over sliced meat and grind pepper over. Turn meat and let stand 20 minutes.

3. In a pan, heat oil over high heat. Add garlic and onion and stir-fry until onion separates and softens. Add cauliflower and mushrooms. Cover, reduce heat and cook for 4 minutes. Add meat and cook until meat until meat is cooked to your liking. Stir in liquid mixture. Continue stirring until sauce thickens. Spoon onto a serving plate and garnish with coriander sprigs.

Serves 4

BAKED PORK LOAF

Ingredients

12 dried mushrooms

8 spring onions, finely chopped

2 tablespoons fish sauce

5 eggs, beaten

pinch salt

ground black pepper

1kg/2lb minced pork

To Garnish:

coriander leaves

Method

1. In hot water, soak mushrooms for 40 minutes then squeeze out liquid, remove stems and chop mushroom tops very finely. Place mushrooms, spring onions and pork in a bowl. Add fish sauce, eggs and salt and pepper to taste and combine thoroughly.

2. Preheat oven to 200°C/400°F. Grease a loaf tin, add meat mixture, patting down firmly. Cover with foil, sealing well. Sit loaf tin in a large roasting pan, pour hot water until half way up the loaf tin and place in oven for about 1 hour or until done. Test with a knife which should come out cleanly.

3. Allow the loaf to cool a little, then run knife around the sides of the tin and turn out. Slice and garnish with coriander.

Serves 6–8

SWEET AND SOUR MEAT BALLS

Ingredients

225g/8oz onions, finely chopped
oil for frying
225g/8oz beef, minced
225g/8oz pork, minced
1 egg, beaten
115g/4oz rice, cooked
extra salt and pepper

Batter:

1 egg
85g/3oz flour
$^2/_3$ cup water

Sweet and Sour Sauce:

55g/2oz onions, finely chopped
2 tablespoons sugar
4 tablespoons dry sherry
2 tablespoons white vinegar
1 cup beef stock
1 cup pineapple juice
4 teaspoons tomato purée
55g/2oz chopped pineapple
1 teaspoon fresh ginger, chopped
1 clove garlic, finely chopped
pinch chilli powder
1 tablespoon arrowroot
water

Method

1. Fry onion, in oil until tender. Drain and add to combination of minced meats, beaten egg and cooked rice. Mix well. Add extra salt and pepper to taste. Form mixture into small balls.

2. Combine batter ingredients. Gently toss balls in seasoned flour. Dip in batter and fry until golden. Drain and set aside.

3. For the sauce, fry onions until tender, add sherry, vinegar, sugar, stock and pineapple juice and boil 6 minutes. Add tomato purée and boil for a further 4 minutes.

4. Purée pineapple, ginger and garlic with a little water and add to sauce along with chilli powder. (Add more to taste if desired.) Blend arrowroot with more water until smooth and add to sauce. Stir until clear and thick, adding more water if too thick. Add meat balls to sauce to heat through before serving.

Serves 4

NOODLE PANCAKE WITH GARLIC BEEF

Ingredients

300g/11oz fillet steak

1/2 red capsicum, seeded and cut into slivers

3 teaspoons minced garlic

6 tablespoons vegetable oil

1/2 teaspoon ground black pepper

400g/14oz fresh, soft noodles

1 tablespoon sugar

1 dessertspoon fish sauce

1/2 cup beef stock

1 dessertspoon cornflour

2 spring onions, chopped

Method

1. Part-freeze steak to make it easier to cut each piece into 2 thin slices. Place steak on a plate and spread with garlic, 1 tablespoon oil and capsicum. Coat with marinade, cover and refrigerate for 45 minutes.

2. Pour 2 1/2 tablespoons oil into a heavy-based pan, ensuring the based is coated. Separate the noodles with your hands. Heat oil to medium, add noodles and press them down with a spatula. Heat until base is golden and crisp. Don't lift the noodle pancake for about 15 minutes as it will break up.

3. Loosen edges and base of pancake gently. Place a large plate over the pan and quickly invert the pan to settle the pancake on the plate. Gently slide the pancake back into the pan, uncooked side down, and continue cooking for 5–10 minutes. Return pancake to plate in the same manner and keep warm in very slow oven.

4. In same pan, heat over high heat 2 1/2 tablespoons oil . Add meat and capsicum mixture and sear quickly on both sides. Don't overcook. Mix sugar, fish sauce, stock and cornflour until smooth and add to steak. Turn meat to absorb flavours, then remove. Stir sauce rapidly until thick, returning steak briefly to coat with sauce.

5. Serve steak and sauce on top of pancake and cut into 4 (or 8 if presenting as an entrée). Top with sauce and garnish with chopped spring onions.

Serves 4 as a main course or 8 as an entrée.

seafood

LUXURY FOR A DONG

Seafood and fish are abundant in Vietnam with its long, curved coastline and its hinterland river systems where freshwater fish are also prolific. Visitors to Vietnam, deprived of shellfish regarded as expensive luxuries in many countries, will find themselves millionaires in Vietnam. This is not just because the currency, the dong, translates into confusing notes worth millions but because visitors can dine so royally on crabs, prawns, shrimp, oysters, mussels and more for a fraction of the cost than at home.

In Vietnam, fish and shellfish, staples next to rice for many (and a great protein injection) are inevitably the first food sources to sell out at sea- and river-port markets.

Because of a general lack of refrigeration, freshness is imperative. Therefore many markets and restaurants offer the choice of live fish swimming in tanks or in plastic buckets. As in Vietnam, freshness is equally important to western cooks. You can assess freshness by checking that scales are not flaky and peeling, eyes are clear and prominent and gills pinked.

And, provided the fruits of the ocean and rivers are not enclosed in thick batter or drenched with rich sauces, they are delights for dieters— especially when prepared in some of the interesting ways to described in the following recipes.

Rarely presented as crumbed calamari, squid is widely appreciated in Vietnam but, at home, avoid over cooking so that its texture does not become rubbery and tough. Soak it overnight in milk.

Sometimes crab can be difficult to buy fresh but crabmeat in a can substitutes well. In dishes where either prawns or shrimp need to be chopped, use either.

Vietnam has several fish not found in western waters so some recipes generalise on the type of fish required. Like the Chinese, Vietnamese are partial to carp which foreigners tend to reject as it is so bony. However, it is a tasty fish when baked and served with a sweet and sour sauce which you'll find in this book.

SALT AND PEPPER SQUID

Ingredients

500g/1 lb squid, cleaned

3 tablespoons self-raising flour

1 tablespoon cornflour

1 tablespoon custard powder or 1 egg

4 tablespoons cold water

vegetable oil for deep-frying

small onion cut into little pieces

1 clove garlic, crushed

2 tablespoons chopped fresh
   parsley or coriander

1 teaspoon sugar

1/2 teaspoon salt

1 1/2 teaspoons ground white pepper

1/2 teaspoon five spice powder

drops of dry sherry (optional)

parsley or coriander sprigs

nuoc cham (page 13)

Method

1. Angle cut squid into square pieces, open up with knife and score each piece with a criss-cross. Dry squid.

2. Make smooth batter of flour, cornflour and custard powder (used to give colour) with water. If using egg for colour, add a little more flour as mixture should not be too runny.

3. Mix batter with squid and cover for a few minutes. Heat oil in wok or frying pan and stir-fry squid for about 3 minutes then remove squid and most of the oil. In remaining oil, place onion and garlic and cook until just tender. Stir in parsley or coriander for 30 seconds. Return squid to pan and sprinkle with combined sugar, salt, pepper and five spice powder. Gently stir through to combine.

4. Toss vermicelli into hot oil for near-instant crispy noodles for the base of a serving plate. Place squid on top, sprinkle a few drops of sherry on top (optional) and garnish with parsley or coriander sprigs. Serve with nuoc cham.

Serves 4

CLAYPOT FISH

Ingredients

370g/13oz freshwater fish,
   cut into bite-sized pieces
115g/4 oz pork loin, sliced
10 cloves garlic, finely chopped
1 cup chicken stock
$\frac{1}{2}$ cup sugar
2 seeded chillis, finely chopped
1 medium onion, sliced
1 tablespoon fish sauce
1 medium tomato, sliced

Method

1. Heat oil in pan. Add fish, and fry lightly until just brown. Transfer fish to a clay pot or stove-top casserole. Brown pork in pan and add to fish along with garlic, stock, sugar and chilli. Stir to combine. Cover and cook on medium heat until sauce is thickened.

2. In pan, sauté onion slices until tender. Add fish sauce to pot and cook, stirring. When pork and fish are cooked, place onions on top. Place fresh tomato on top just before serving.

Serves 4

PRAWN CURRY

Ingredients

2 tablespoons vegetable oil

2 cloves garlic, finely chopped

12 king prawns, cooked

1 onion, sliced

1 medium zucchini, sliced

1/2 green capsicum, seeded and sliced

1/2 tablespoon green curry paste

1 cup coconut milk

1 teaspoon cornflour

1 tablespoon water

1 teaspoon sugar

1 tablespoon fish sauce

To Garnish:

coriander leaves

Method

1. Heat oil in pan. Add garlic and prawns and stir-fry for 2 minutes. Add onion, zucchini and capsicum, stirring for 2 more minutes. Remove from stove.

2. In another pan, place curry paste and stir constantly for 1 minute. Add coconut milk and bring to the boil. Mix cornflour with water. Add sugar, fish sauce and cornflour mixture. Add prawns with vegetables. Garnish with coriander leaves and serve with steamed rice.

Serves 4

CHILLI CRAB WITH LEMONGRASS

Ingredients

1 large crab (1 1/3 kg/3lb) or 2 smaller crabs

1 tablespoon oil

2 cloves garlic, finely chopped

1 onion, sliced

1 stalk lemongrass, finely sliced

4 chillies, sliced

2 tablespoons fish sauce

2 tablespoons lime juice

1/2 cup water

4 spring onions, cut into 2 1/2 cm/1 in pieces

1/2 cup bean shoots

deep-fried shallots

extra lime juice and fish sauce, for serving

Method

1. Clean the crab well. Heat oil in a large saucepan, stir-fry garlic, onion, lemongrass and chilli over high heat for a few minutes.

2. Pour fish sauce, lime juice and water into the pan and bring to the boil. Carefully place crab in saucepan. Cover with a tightly fitting lid. Cook over a medium high heat for 10–15 minutes until the crab is cooked.

3. Place crab on a serving platter. Add spring onions to the pan, reduce cooking liquid to about 1/4 cup and pour over the crab.

4. Arrange bean shoots over the hot crab, sprinkle liberally with deep-fried shallots and serve with extra lime juice and fish sauce.

Serves 2–4

BARBECUED PRAWNS

Ingredients

500g/1 lb large green prawns
170g/6oz thin vermicelli
   boiling water
2 teaspoons vegetable oil
6 green shallots, chopped
1/2 cup/75g/21/2oz roasted peanuts
1/2 bunch coriander leaves, chopped
nuoc cham(see page 13)

Method

1. Slit prawns down back, remove vein, wash and pat dry. Cook prawns over charcoal for about 5 minutes, turning once.

2. Add rice vermicelli to boiling water and boil for 2 minutes. Drain and rinse under cold running water.

3. Heat oil in wok or frying pan, add green shallots and fry until softened. Arrange on warmed serving plates, top with prawns, then sprinkle with shallots and peanuts. Pour hot nuoc cham over top and sprinkle with chopped coriander.

Serves 4

HANOI-STYLE FRIED FISH
(opposite)

Ingredients
2 tablespoons shrimp paste
   with soya bean oil

$1/4$ cup fish sauce

1 tablespoon sugar

500g/1 lb boneless fish fillets

salt and pepper

$1/4$ cup peanut oil

4 teaspoons grated tumeric

1 heaped teaspoon ginger, grated

4 spring onions, chopped

$1/2$ cup fresh dill, chopped

2 tablespoons crushed peanuts

nuoc cham

To Garnish:

lettuce and mint leves

Method
1. Prepare nuoc cham by mixing shrimp paste, a little extra oil, fish sauce and sugar. Boil and add more sugar if desired.

2. Season fish with salt and pepper and cut into 2.5cm/1in pieces. In a heavy-based pan, heat oil, then add fish, turmeric and ginger. Turn gently and just before fish is done, add spring onions, dill and peanuts. Serve, with dipping sauce lettuce and mint on a bed of rice.

Serves 4

NHA TRANG EEL

Ingredients
1 eel, about 1kg/2lbs

10 black dried mushrooms

$1/2$ green capsicum, seeded

$1/2$ cup liquid from pineapple pieces

oil for cooking

2 cloves garlic, crushed

2 onions, sliced

1 dessertspoon fish sauce

ground black pepper

1 cup canned pineapple pieces

2 large tomatoes, cut into small wedges

1 dessertspoon cornflour

To Garnish:

parsley

Method
1. Wash eel, peel it, remove back bone and cut into bite-sized pieces. Soak mushrooms in boiling water for 30 minutes then remove and discard stems. Cut capsicum into 2.5cm/1in squares. Reserve $1/2$ cup liquid when draining pineapple.

2. Heat oil in pan over medium heat and fry garlic and onions until soft. Add eel, capsicum, fish sauce and a sprinkle of pepper to taste. Stir-fry until eel has softened, adding more oil if necessary. Add pineapple pieces, tomatoes and mushrooms, stirring to heat through.

3. Combine cornflour with pineapple juice and add to pan. Serve when sauce is thickened. Garnish with parsley.

Serves 4–6

CRAB MEAT BOATS

Ingredients
3 eggplants

3 spring onions, chopped

oil for cooking

$1 1/2$ cups cooked or canned crabmeat

coriander sprigs, to garnish

Sauce:

2 small, red chillis, seeded and minced

2 tablespoons peanuts, crushed

$1/4$ cup fish sauce

1 teaspoon sugar

3 tablespoons water

Method
1. Halve eggplants lengthwise and brush with oil. Barbecue or grill, turning frequently until flesh softens completely and skin darkens. Carefully peel off skins and discard but retain split stem for decorative purpose. Keep eggplant boats warm.

2. Fry two thirds of spring onions in oil until golden. Add sauce ingredients, cook until sugar is dissolved then add crab meat and heat through.

3. Place eggplant boats on one large or individual plates. Spoon over equal amounts of crab meat and sauce and garnish with remaining chopped spring onion and coriander sprigs.

Note: Cooked, chopped or small, whole shrimps can substitute for crab meat
if desired.

Serves 6 as an appetiser, or
3 as a main course.

SQUID CHA (CAKES)

Ingredients

2 tablespoons pork fat, finely chopped

1 dessertspoon dry sherry

pinch salt

1 teaspoon sugar

2 teaspoons ground pepper

1 small seeded orange chilli seeded
   and finely chopped

500g/1 lb squid, finely chopped

2 tablespoons parsley, chopped

3 spring onions, chopped

3 teaspoons fish sauce

1 egg

vegetable oil

Sauce:

2 teaspoons fish sauce

2 teaspoons lime or lemon juice or vinegar

2 teaspoons sugar

3 teaspoons water

To Garnish:

1 lime

$^1/_2$ red capsicum, seeded

$^1/_2$ cucumber

coriander sprigs

Method

1. Boil pork fat to soften then finely chop again. Add sherry, salt, sugar and pepper. Place in a warm place to soften further.

2. Meanwhile, reserve a pinch of chopped chilli for sauce. Add the remainder to squid with parsley and spring onions. Put fish sauce in pot and heat until pot is nearly dry (to flavour it) and add any crystals to squid.

3. Separate egg and lightly beat white and yolk in individual bowls. Combine pork fat mixture with squid and add enough egg white to bind. Oil your hands and make flat cakes of squid. Lightly fry in wok or frypan, turning in oil, adding more oil as necessary. Cakes will expand. Remove squid cakes and allow to cool. Wipe wok or pan clean with kitchen paper. Dip cakes in egg yolk to give yellow colour and re-fry in more fresh oil.

4. Combine sauce ingredients with reserved chilli. Slowly heat until sugar is dissolved.

5. Thinly slice lime and capsicum. Halve lime rings and arrange in a circle on a plate with thin slices of cucumber. Add hot squid cakes, pour sauce over and garnish with coriander sprigs.

Serves 4

chicken & poultry

CHICK OUT
FOR A DUCK

One has only to stroll through a market in Hanoi, Saigon or one of hundreds of villages and towns between the major Vietnamese cities to realise how popular poultry is with the Vietnamese.

Strung up in busy meat sections, plump, live and feathered in wicker cages, chicken is chosen carefully for its versatility and economy over red meat.

In some of Vietnam's most picturesque regions of bizarrely shaped rocky outcrops dominating rice paddies, ducks are farmed and are noisy, moving foregrounds against stunning scenery. Raised in healthy conditions, ducks are also revered in the kitchen for their adaptability. While meat, poultry and fish are not eaten every day in households, duck and chicken are the most favoured meats next to pork.

Almost every part of the bird is used, even its feet which, some believe, uplift the spirit. Chicken and duck feet are favourites of young women who eat them when they need personal pampering.

The Greeks regard the bull's testicles as a delicacy that ecourages virility. Vietnam has a similar philosophy except the balls are not from the bull. The proud, strutting rooster's genitalia is the 'test' treat – and tasty too, but not included in our recipes. If they're available and you're intrigued, prepare rooster testes sautéed, with a sweet and sour sauce with diced ham and peas added.

In salads, roasts, grills, stir fries, slow cook pots, fricasses, curries and appetisers, poultry makes constant appearances and frequently replaces seafood when diners are allergic to shellfish.

Indeed, few dishes including seafood in this book, are not amenable to preparation with chicken instead. Some recipes exude certain distinguishable influences of former occupying and neighboring countries.

As in other Asian countries, butchering is imprecise to western eyes. So if you have a cleaver, become a hack

STIR-FRIED LEMON GRASS CHICKEN

Ingredients

4 stalks lemon grass

500g/18oz skinless boneless chicken breasts,
    cut into 2¹/₂cm/1in cubes

1 teaspoon sesame oil

2 tablespoon vegetable oil

1 red capsicum, deseeded and chopped

2 tablespoons roasted salted peanuts,
    roughly chopped

1 tablespoon fish sauce

1 tablespoon soy sauce

¹/₂ tablespoon sugar

salt

2 spring onions, chopped

Method

1. Peel the outer layers from lemon grass stalks and finely chop the lower white bulbous parts, discarding the fibrous tops. Put chicken into a large bowl, add lemon grass and sesame oil and turn to coat. Cover and marinate in the fridge for 2 hours, or overnight.

2. Heat a wok or large, heavy-based frying pan, and add vegetable oil. Add chicken with its marinade and stir-fry for 5 minutes or until the chicken has turned white.

3. Add red pepper, peanuts, fish sauce, soy sauce, sugar and salt to taste. Stir-fry for another 5 minutes or until chicken and pepper are cooked. Sprinkle with the spring onions just before serving.

Serves 4

SPICY ORANGE DUCK

Ingredients

2kg/4¼lb duck pieces

vegetable oil

3 tablespoons sugar

2 cups orange juice

2 oranges

finely sliced orange rind

2 small red chillis, seeded and sliced

Marinade:

3 tablespoons fish sauce

1 tablespoon peeled ginger, finely chopped

1 tablespoon red chilli,
   seeded and finely chopped

salt and pepper

1 tablespoon vegetable oil

Method

1. Combine marinade ingredients, coat both sides of duck pieces and marinate, preferably overnight.

2. Heat oil in pan, add duck pieces along with marinade and cook until golden. Turn pieces and baste. Turn heat down a little. When duck is almost cooked, sprinkle half the sugar over. When time to turnagain, sprinkle with rest of sugar. While sugar is becoming caramel, add orange juice, stir and remove duck pieces.

3. Peel oranges, divide into segments and arrange on serving plate. Add duck. Stir orange sauce until it reaches desired thickness. Pour sauce over duck pieces and decorate with orange rind slices and extra chillis.

Serves 6

CHICKEN WITH CAULIFLOWER

Ingredients

2 large chicken fillets

2 cloves garlic, minced

salt and ground black pepper, to taste

4 tablespoons vegetable oil

2 large onions, each cut into 8

2 cups small cauliflower florets

1 red chilli, seeded and chopped

Sauce:

2 tablespoons cornflour

1 cup chicken stock
   (powdered or cube will do)

1 dessertspooon soy sauce

1 tablespoon vinegar

1 tablespoon fish sauce

Method

1. Between 2 sheets of plastic film, pound chicken until thin. Slice into thin strips to make almost 2 cups. Season with garlic, salt and plenty of pepper. Stir and set aside for 10 minutes.

2. Heat pan, add 2 tablespoons oil and sauté chicken quickly. Remove from pan. Reheat pan, add remaining oil and sauté onion until brown but not cooked. Add cauliflower florets and chilli and sauté for a further 10–15 minutes.

3. Mix cornflour with vinegar and sauces until smooth. Add to cup of stock.

4. Combine chicken with vegetables, add sauce and stir as the mixture thickens. Serve with steamed rice or noodles.

Note: Thin rare beef strips can replace chicken.

Serves 4

duck

HONEY ROASTED DUCK

Ingredients

3 teaspoons ground black pepper
3 teaspoons salt
3 tablespoons sugar
2½ tablespoons peanut oil
1 medium to large whole duck
6 tablespoons honey
6 tablespoons light soy sauce
2 tablespoons lime or lemon juice
pinch saffron or turmeric (optional)

To Garnish:

tomatoes, thinly sliced
cucumber, thinly sliced
1 red chilli, seeded and sliced
coriander

Method

1. Combine together pepper, salt, sugar and 4 teaspoons of oil. Rub duck inside and out and seal flavours inside by securing the opening with a bamboo skewer. Preheat oven to 190°C/370°F.

2. Mix honey, soy sauce, lime or lemon juice, remaining 2 teaspoons of oil and optional saffron or turmeric used for its colour rather than flavour. Pour over duck, ensuring it reaches the whole surface (a must) every 10 minutes. Place in oven and bast until duck is golden and cooked through.

3. Cut up into serving pieces, and garnish with tomatoes, cucumber, chilli and coriander sprigs.

Note: Chicken, quails, goat and rabbit or other game may replace duck.

Serves 6–8

SPICY CHICKEN SKEWERS

Ingredients

1 kg/2 lb boneless chicken fillets

Marinade:

2 spring onions, chopped

1 stalk lemongrass, peeled and finely sliced

2½ tablespoons sugar

1 small, seeded red chilli, crushed

1 tablespoon fish sauce

1 tablespoon soy sauce

1 tablespoon peanut oil

1 tablespoon coconut milk

1½ teaspoons five spice powder

nuoc cham (see page 13)

peanut sauce (see page 62)

Method

1. Soak about 25 bamboo skewers in water overnight or in boiling water for at least 45 minutes so they will not burn when cooking. Combine marinade ingredients.

2. Cut chicken into thin strips, add to marinade, ensuring each strip is covered. Cover and refrigerate several hours or overnight.

3. Drain chicken and discard marinade. Thread chicken strips on to skewers. Barbecue or grill for about 3 minutes until brown.

4. Serve as part of a main course or as an appetiser with nuoc cham or peanut sauce

Makes 20–25

TURKEY WITH MUSHROOMS

Ingredients

1 cup dried mushrooms

1½kg/3½lb turkey hindquarter

2½ teaspoons vegetable oil

2 tablespoons soy sauce

2 tablespoons dry sherry

3 teaspoons sugar

peel from 1½ oranges

salt and pepper, to taste

To Garnish:

mint sprigs

Method

1. Soak mushrooms in boiling water for 30 minutes. Drain and discard stems. Slice.

2. Chop turkey hindquarter into chunks, using a cleaver to get through the bone. Pour boiling water over pieces to fatten skin then drain and dry with kitchen paper. Brown turkey, over a medium heat, in just enough oil to cover a heavy-based pan. Cook in batches, wiping pan clean with kitchen paper after each batch and adding more oil as necessary.

3. To a clean pan add fresh oil and return turkey along with soy sauce, sherry, sugar, mushrooms and peel from 1 orange. Bring to the boil.

4. Turn heat down to simmer, cover and cook, stirring and skimming scum from surface occasionally, until turkey is tender. Season with salt and pepper, remove from heat and stand covered for 5 minutes. Discard orange peel and serve topped with sauce. Garnish with peel from remaining ½ orange and mint.

Note: Chicken or duck can be used in this recipe.

Serves 6

CHICKEN EGG CAKES

Ingredients

55g/2oz cellophane noodles

4 dried mushrooms

2 cloves garlic, minced

1 tablespoon vegetable oil

6 eggs

400g/14oz chicken fillet, minced

1½ teaspoons sugar

pinch salt

ground black pepper

2 teaspooons fresh coriander, finely chopped

To Garnish:

1 spring onion, sliced

6 sprigs coriander

nuoc cham (see page 13)

soy sauce

Method

1. Soak noodles in boiling water for 10 minutes. Chop into 2cm/³⁄₄in sections. Soak mushrooms in boiling water for 10 minutes, drain and slice. Soften garlic in oil over medium heat. Pre-heat oven to 150°C/300°F.

2. In a bowl, beat eggs and add garlic, chicken, noodles, mushrooms, sugar, coriander and salt and pepper to taste. Combine thoroughly and pour into lightly greased heatproof soup bowls or one large bowl.

3. Place bowls in a baking dish and fill it half way with water. Cover bowls and steam (for 10–15 minutes) or until cakes are set. Remove lids for just long enough for top turn golden. Garnish with spring onions and a sprig of coriander. Serve with separate bowls of nuoc cham and soy sauce.

Note: Minced pork, beef, prawns or crabmeat can be used instead of chicken.

Serves 4–6, depending on depth of bowl.

vegetables

FRESH, DRIED, COOKED IN A PICKLE

Where rice paddies do not carpet the landscape, and no animals graze, vegetables grow. Vegetable crops are mixed on farms and certainly in the countryside, where most small dwellings have little gardens. But, as many city Vietnamese inhabit apartments or sparse rooms without space to garden, and poverty is widespread, vegies from the market are more popular than meat (even though the majority of Vietnamese love meat). Markets offer a great choice of vegetables which are selected carefully as the Vietnamese are fussy about freshness.

As the rural areas of neighbouring countries, lack of refrigeration often means marke shopping is done twice daily by the home cook. Block ice is still sold by some vendors but it's usually sold by the bucketful to be shaved to cool warm beer. Ice is a dubious water source for visiting beer or smoothie drinkers the juices in Vietnamese smoothies are mixed with coconut milk or canned sweetened condensed milk. Savoury smoothies are likely to contain chilli and, guess what? Coriander.

Metropolitan Asian markets or stores will have good selections of dried (to be reconstituted), canned and packaged vegetable ingredients if vegetables are unavailable fresh.

Chillis, pineapples, tomatoes, asparagus and avocados were introduced to Vietnam over the centuries and will never be relinquished. Preserved vegetables are sold in small containers in Asian food stores and markets but are used sparingly to flavour rice or noodles or to add flavours to soups and stews. The taste is piquantly biting.

Tofu or beancurd, made from soy beans, is widely used. Visiting vegans will never go hungry but they should try to check that fish or oyster sauce or shrimp paste has not been used in the preparation of a vegetable dish.

SPINACH WITH PEANUT SAUCE

Ingredients
750g/1 1/2 lb water spinach or mature spinach
3 spring onions, sliced
2 cloves garlic, crushed
1 1/2 tablespoons vegetable oil
1/4 cup peanuts, crushed
salt and pepper

Peanut Sauce:
1/3 cup smooth peanut butter
1/2 cup coconut milk
1 1/2 tablespoons sugar
1/3 cup sweet chilli sauce
2 teaspoons lime or lemon juice
1/3 cup vegetable stock

To Garnish:
coriander springs

Method
1. Trim stalks of water spinach. Blanch spinach in boiling water to make limp then place in cool or iced water. Drain completely.

2. Make peanut sauce in saucepan by combining all ingredients and stirring over low heat until smooth.

3. Fry spring onions and garlic in oil until tender. Add peanuts and then spinach and peanut sauce. Season with salt and pepper and garnish with coriander.

Serves 4

POTATO PATTIES

Ingredients

2 large, old potatoes, peeled

pinch salt

$^1/_4$ cup cornflour

1 large egg

3 spring onions, chopped

1 small onion, minced

3 cloves garlic, minced

2 teaspoons fish sauce

2 teaspoons curry powder

ground black pepper

$^2/_3$ cup vegetable oil

nuoc cham (see page 13)

Method

1. Grate potato or shred in a food processor. Put in a colander, sprinkle with salt and mix though. Let stand 20 minutes then squeeze out natural liquid. Place in a bowl and combine with cornflour.

2. Beat egg lightly and add it to potato along with remaining ingredients, except the oil. Combine well. Heat oil in a large heavy-based pan. Ladle in potato mixture by the tablespoon. Patties should be about 6cm/2$^1/_2$in diameter.

3. Fry until golden (about 4 minutes) turn and when each patty is crisp, drain on kitchen paper. Serve hot with nuoc cham.

Note: Taro roots or sweet potatoes can be substituted.

Serves 4 as a main course accompaniment.

CURRIED VEGETABLES

Ingredients

115g/4oz carrots
115g/4oz green beans
255g/9oz new potatoes, peeled and quartered
1 eggplant
2 stalks lemongrass
2½ tablespoons vegetable oil
2 spring onions, thinly sliced
3 cloves garlic, crushed
3 tablespoons curry powder
2 teaspoons shrimp paste (optional)
2 dried red chillis, chopped
1 cup vegetable stock
1 cup coconut milk
1 tablespoon fish sauce
2 lime leaves or strips of lime or lemon peel
salt

Method

1. Prepare vegetables. Remove outer leaves and trim ends and tough tops of lemongrass. Slice as finely as possible. Trim beans. Peel carrots and cut both diagonally into 3½cm/1½in pieces. Slice eggplant into 2½cm/1in rounds, salt and let stand 10 minutes then drain liquid and quarter each round.

2. Heat oil in a heavy-based pan, add spring onions and garlic and sauté until just golden. Add curry powder, shrimp paste if desired, lemongrass and chillis and cook about 6 minutes. Add stock, coconut milk, fish sauce and lime leaves or citrus peel. Cover and bring to the boil.

3. Reduce heat to medium, add carrots, potatoes, beans and eggplant. Part-cover and simmer until vegetables are tender and liquid has reduced. Season with salt

Serves 4

STEAMED STUFFED CUCUMBERS

Ingredients

4 black dried mushrooms

500g/1 lb cucumber

1½ teaspoons cornflour

375g/12oz canned water chestnuts

2½ tablespoons glutinous rice flour

sesame oil

½ teaspoon sugar

½ teaspoon salt

4 tablespoons cooked, diced carrot

vegetable oil

pepper

¾ cup stock or water

Method

1. Soak mushrooms for 30 minutes, drain then remove and discard stalks, and chop the remainder.

2. Thinly peel cucumbers and cut into 1cm/½in pieces. Scrape flesh out and discard. Parboil cucumber shells for 1 minute. Rinse in cold water, drain and dust inside with a little cornflour.

3. Drain water chestnuts and discard liquid. Mash and add rice flour, a dash of sesame oil and ¼ teaspoon each of sugar and salt. Add carrot and mushrooms and mix well. Stuff cucumber circles and place on a plate to steam, covered, for 15 minutes.

4. In a separate saucepan, mix a dash of oil with pepper to taste and remaining sugar and salt. Add remaining cornflour. Stir in stock or water until smooth. Heat until thickened and pour over the cooked cucumber pieces.

Serves 4–6

HERBED RICE NOODLES WITH ASPARAGUS AND PEANUTS

Ingredients

3 tablespoons rice vinegar

1 tablespoon sugar

1 small Spanish onion, finely sliced

255g/9oz dried rice noodles

2 bunches of asparagus

$^1/_3$ cup chopped fresh mint

$^1/_3$ cup chopped fresh coriander

1 continental cucumber, peeled,
    seeded and thinly sliced

6 spring onions, finely sliced

3 Roma tomatoes, finely diced

$^3/_4$ cup roasted peanuts, lightly crushed

juice of 2 limes

2 teaspoons fish sauce

2 teaspoons olive oil

$^1/_2$ teaspoon chilli flakes

Method

1. Whisk rice vinegar and sugar together and pour over the finely sliced onion rings. Allow to marinate for 1 hour, tossing frequently.

2. Cook noodles according to packet directions. (Usually, rice noodles need only to soak in boiling water for 5 minutes, otherwise, boil for 1–2 minutes then drain immediately and rinse under cold water.)

3. Cut off the tough stalks of the asparagus, and cut remaining stalks into 2cm/$^3/_4$in lengths. Simmer asparagus in salted water for 2 minutes until bright green and crisp-tender. Rinse in cold water to refresh.

4. Toss noodles with reserved onion and vinegar mixture while still warm then, using kitchen scissors, cut noodles into manageable lengths.

5. Add the cooked asparagus to noodles along with chopped mint, coriander, cucumber, spring onions, tomatoes and roasted peanuts and toss thoroughly.

6. Whisk lime juice, fish sauce, oil and chilli flakes together and drizzle over the noodle salad. Serve at room temperature.

Serves 4

TOFU STUFFED TOMATOES

Ingredients

6 large, firm tomatoes
1/2 cup firm tofu, drained
1 cup fresh mushrooms, chopped
3 cloves garlic, minced
4 spring onions, chopped
1 tablespoon fish sauce
1 teaspoon ground white pepper
1 egg, beaten
1 tablespoon cornflour
1/4 cup vegetable oil

To Garnish:

1/4 cup coriander, chopped

Method

1. Cut tops from tomatoes, remove core, pulp and set aside. Mash tofu and mix in a bowl with mushrooms, garlic, spring onions, fish sauce, pepper, egg and cornflour. Fill tomatoes with the mixture.

2. Heat oil in a large frying pan over high heat then carefully add tomatoes, stuffed side down. Cook for about 4 minutes, turn to low and cook for another 6 minutes.

3. Serve garnished with coriander and with sweet and sour sauce (see page 39)

Serves 6.

STICKY RICE WITH BEANSPROUTS

Ingredients

255g/9oz glutinous rice

water

225g/8oz fresh bean sprouts or mung dhal

pinch salt

Method

1. Cover rice with water. If not using fresh bean sprouts, soak mung dhal in water in a separate bowl. Leave both to soak overnight then wash rice and mung dhal until water runs clear. Mix rice and mung dhal with salt.

2. Line a bamboo steamer or top of a metal steamer with a tea towel, or greaseproof paper and spread rice and mung dhal over it. Cover with folded sides of tea towel and/or lid. Steam for about 40 minutes, replenishing water, until cooked. If using fresh bean sprouts, add to cooked rice and fluff through with a fork.

Note: For plain sticky rice, steam as above (without bean sprouts or boil) 4 cups of water to 2 cups of soaked glutinous rice, for 10 minutes. Remove from heat, drain, cover and stand for 15 minutes.

Serves 6

salads

RIPE FOR EXPERIMENTS

Vietnamese salads differ from many in the world in that they often include seafoods or meats. For westerners this makes the salads light, nutritious, main courses when served with crusty bread. So refreshing in summer. In Vietnam, salads come as part of a multi-course meal but, visitors to Vietnam should be wary if the fresh, raw ingredients have been washed in bottled water.

With tropical to cool-climate fruits, herbs and vegetables growing in Vietnam's varying conditions and temperatures, colorful salads reflect different flavors and textures and are ripe for experimentation if certain ingredients are unavailable. For example, Madame Do Minh Thu's Green papaya salad with shrimps and pork should be a Banana blossom salad. If the daikon, (large white radish) can't be found, use red-skinned radish.

Vegetarians can omit meats and certain sauces from the following salads. Some dressings here will add exciting new flavours to familiar, home-prepared salad favourites.

SAIGON SALAD

Ingredients
8 cooked potatoes
400g/14oz can artichoke hearts
400g/14oz can button mushrooms

Dressing:
4 tablespoons white vinegar
juice of $^1/_2$ lemon
$^1/_4$ cup parsley, chopped
large pinch dried dill
salt to taste
ground black pepper

To Garnish:
parsley sprigs walnuts, quartered

Method
1. Peel potatoes, slice and place in salad bowl. Combine dressing ingredients well and pour over potatoes.

2. Drain artichokes and mushrooms and discard liquid. Carefully mix with potatoes and dressing and garnish with walnuts and parsley.

Serves 4

GREEN PAPAYA SALAD

Ingredients

750g/26oz green papaya, finely julienned
4 spring onions, very finely julienned
half white radish, very finely julienned
12 Asian mint leaves
12 Thai basil (or regular basil) leaves
¼ bunch coriander, leaves only
1 clove garlic, minced

Dressing:

¼ teaspoon shrimp paste
2 tablespoons boiling water
3 tablespoons rice vinegar
3 tablespoons lime juice
2 tablespoons fish sauce
2 tablespoons sugar
1 tablespoon sweet chilli sauce

To Garnish:

2 tablespoons dried shrimp or crushed peanuts
extra Thai basil and Asian mint leaves

Method

1. Toss papaya with spring onions, white radish, chopped fresh herbs and garlic.

2. To make the dressing, dilute shrimp paste in boiling water, then whisk with all other dressing ingredients. If the sauce is a little too acidic, add a little extra water to dilute the flavour to your taste. Continue whisking until the dressing is well mixed.

3. Toss dressing through papaya and vegetable mixture, taking care to disperse the dressing thoroughly.

4. Pile onto a plate and sprinkle with peanuts or dried shrimp.

Serves 8

CHICKEN SALAD

Ingredients

1 onion, finely sliced

1 carrot, cut in julienne strips

1 radish, finely sliced

1 stick celery, finely sliced

$^1/_2$ green or red capsicum,
  seeded and finely sliced

2 cups cooked chicken, chopped

1 cup lettuce leaves, torn

$^1/_4$ quarter cucumber,
  sliced diagonally

Dressing:

5 tablespoons lemon juice

$^1/_3$ cup water

3 tablespoons sugar

To Garnish:

1 tablespoon mint, chopped

1 small seeded red chilli, sliced

Method

1. Mix dressing ingredients.
   Combine salad vegetables except
   lettuce and cucumbe in a bowl.
   Pour over dressing, cover and
   refrigerate for 1 hour. Transfer to
   a salad bowl.

2. Add chicken, lettuce and
   cucumber, toss together and
   sprinkle with mint and chilli rings.

Serves 4

desserts

SWEET
SNACKING

Vietnamese dessert, following a family home meal, is inevitably fruit since the country is blessed with so many varieties of fruit. Fruits include bananas, watermelon, mangosteen, jackfruit, mango, guava, pineapple, pomelo (like grapefruit), rambutan, custard apple, lychees, tamarind, durian and more. Readers in tropical regions will have little difficulty in obtaining most of these fruits.

The French made a big impact on the creation of desserts in Vietnam. This may relieve visitors hankering for more than fruit pieces. Sweetmeats, including *che* (made from green mung beans) cakes, cookies and desserts are snack foods, bought between meals from hawkers, market stalls and Gaelic-style patisseries.

The Vietnamese have adapted many well appreciated French recipes in several ways. One adaption is to replace milk and cream with respectively, coconut milk and cream. These ingredients add refreshing flavours and are essentially lower in cholesterol and kilojoulesthan the dairy equivalents. Quaintly, some desserts, such as the créme caramel to follow, are called flans when no pastry is evident. Dessert soups are also unusual but very cooling in summer.

Although the habit in Vietnam is to serve all lunch and dinner dishes together around the rice pot, without dessert, break the tradition with a triumphantly sweet finale to your own Vietnamese dinner party. If, in Vietnam, a host offers *banh* (meaning cake), don't necessarily expect a rich gateau – although you may get it. The term 'cake' covers all sorts of sweet and savoury treats, from vegetable rolls and seafood rice crepes to fruity tarts.

GINGER BISCUITS

Ingredients
125g/4¹/₂oz plain flour
125g/4¹/₂oz caster sugar
¹/₄ teaspoon bicarbonate of soda
pinch salt
2 tablespoons ground ginger
1 teaspoon ground cinnamon
55g/2oz butter
1 tablespooon golden syrup
1 small egg

Method
1. Pre-heat oven to 170°C/325°F. Sift flour, sugar, bi-carb and salt into a bowl. Add ginger and cinnamon. Work butter in with hands until texture of breadcrumbs. Beat golden syrup and egg together and gradully add to flour mix to form dough.

2. Form into small balls and place well apart on to greased baking trays. Bake until crisply golden.

Makes about 20 biscuits

COCONUT FLAN WITH CARAMEL (CRÉME CARAMEL)

Ingredients

Caramel:

¹/₄ cup sugar

¹/₄ cup hot water

Custard:

1 cup fresh, canned or
   reconstituted powdered coconut milk

1 cup milk

¹/₄ cup sugar

4 eggs

1 teaspoon vanilla essence

mint sprig, to decorate

Method

1. To make caramel melt sugar alone in a small, heavy pot, over a low heat. Swirl the pot constantly until the sugar becomes golden. Stir in hot water carefully as the mixture will splatter. Quickly stir to dissolve any lumps and boil for about 2 minutes until liquid is clear.

2. Pour caramel into a 4 cups/1¹/₂pint soufflé dish which has been lightly greased with butter or margarine. Tilt the dish to ensure caramel coats the base.

3. To make custard, beat eggs and vanilla in a large bowl. Combine coconut milk and milk with sugar in a saucepan and cook over low heat until sugar dissolves. Remove from stove and beat quickly into eggs and vanilla so eggs do not curdle. Sieve custard only if it is lumpy. Pour slowly on top of caramel in soufflé dish.

4. Pre-heat oven to 160°C/325°F. In the base of a large roasting pan, place 2 layers of paper towelling, then place the soufflé dish on top before pouring hot water into the roasting pan until half way up the soufflé dish. Bake in the centre of the oven for about 50 minutes or until a knife inserted into custard is clean when removed. Do not allow water to boil. Remove soufflé. Cool in a pan of cold water. Chill, covered with plastic wrap, preferably overnight.

5. To serve, run a knife around the circumference of the dish and place a dinner plate on top. In a quick movement, invert the dish and the créme caramel will slide onto the plate. Serve alone or with whipped cream. Place a mint sprig in the centre to garnish.

Serves 6

MANGO CAKE WITH NUTMEG CREAM

Ingredients

1 cup unsalted, roasted macadamia nuts

3 large mangoes, about 750g/26oz

255g/9oz butter, softened

1 teaspoon vanilla essence

1 cup caster sugar

4 large eggs

2 cups plain flour

1½ teaspoons baking powder

½ cup roasted macadamia nuts, chopped

icing sugar

2 cups pure cream

1 teaspoon nutmeg

1 mango, sliced, for serving

Method

1. Preheat the oven to 180°C/350°F and grease a 22cm/9in non-stick cake tin with butter.

2. Crush roasted macadamia nuts in a food processor and set aside.

3. Peel mangoes and dice the flesh, saving as much juice as possible, then reserve some nice pieces of mango (about 85g/3oz) and purée the remaining mango flesh with all the reserved juice. You should have about 1 cup of mango purée.

4. Beat softened butter and vanilla essence with half the sugar. Beat until thick and pale. While beating, add remaining sugar and beat until all sugar has been added. Add eggs, one at a time, and beat well after each addition.

5. In a separate bowl, combine crushed nuts, flour and baking powder.

6. Remove the bowl from the mixer and add the flour mixture, stirring well to combine. Add the mango purée and mix gently.

7. Spoon the batter into the prepared tin, then sprinkle chopped macadamia nuts and reserved diced mango over the batter and swirl through.

8. Bake for 1 hour, then remove the cake from the oven and cool in the tin. When cool, remove from the tin and dredge with icing sugar.

9. To prepare the cream, whip cream and nutmeg together until the cream is thick and fragrant. Serve alongside the cake with some mango slices.

Serves 6

ALMOND RICE JELLY

Ingredients

85g/3oz ground rice
170g/6oz ground almonds
55g/2oz powdered gelatine
170g/6oz caster sugar
55g/2oz desiccated coconut
4¹/₂ cups boiling water
few drops of almond essence

Method

1. Mix together all dried ingredients. Add boiling water, while stirring and bring to the boil. Simmer, still stirring, for 10 minutes until thick. Stir in almond essence. Pour into lightly greased serving bowl, cool, cover and refrigerate.

2. Serve with a bowl of canned lychees, gooseberries or fresh guava and cream if desired.

Serves 4

GINGER MELON SOUP

Ingredients

1 rock melon (about 750g/26oz)
55g/2oz ginger, peeled
3½ cups water
100g/3½oz sugar
315g/11oz glass noodles
juice of 2 limes or lemons

Method

1. Peel melon, remove seeds, cut into small cubes and machine-blend. Keep cool. Slice ginger finely and boil half of it in water with half the sugar until dissolved. Turn heat down, add noodles to simmer for 5 minutes. Remove from heat, allow to cool, pour into a bowl, remove ginger and chill.

2. In a saucepan, boil together remaining sugar, ginger and lime or lemon juice. Simmer until thick. Remove from heat, cool and remove ginger. Chill.

3. In individual bowls set in larger ice-filled bowls, pour equal quantities of gingered melon purée. Top with noodles then lime or lemon mix. Garnish each with a mint leaf and serve with ginger biscuits to dunk and soften.

Serves 4

Baguette: Crusty bread stick introduced by the French.

Bamboo Shoots: Savoury, crunchy vegetable. Sold in cans in the West.

Banana leaves: Flavourless leaves used for wrapping rolls. Use foil if unavailable

Basil: Herb which as a faint aniseed flavour. Used as an ingredient or garnish

Beancurd: Aka tofu, low in fat, no cholesterol, made from soybean. Available soft, semi-soft and firm. A versatile meat replacement.

Bean sprouts: Mung bean sprouts, raw in salads, also a savoury ingredient. Can be grown in cotton wool at home.

Black bean sauce: Fermented soy beans with wheat flour and water.

Cabbage: Versatile leaves that have a delicate sweet aroma with a mild cabbage flavour. Substitute for banana blossom in salads and cooked dishes.

Cane sugar: Gives sugar explosion when sucked. Juice is a popular drink.

Can: Thin bamboo straw for drinking moonshine of same name. Made from rice.

Chao: Rice porridge.

Chay: Vegetarian.

Che: Sweetmeat of mung beans. Cakes available at dessert shops

Chillis: Red or green, mildly hot ingredient and garnish. A fiery seasoning also available powdered (hot) and flaked.

Coconut: Desiccated, use as dry ingredient or with boiling water doubled in quantity, mix, cool, squeeze and strain through sieve for coconut cream or add more water for milk; coconut cream and milk are available in cartons, canned or powdered for reconstitution.

Com: Means rice; also simple eating place.

Coriander: Aka Chinese parsley; indispensable fresh in Vietnamese dishes; dried no substitute for fresh; also called cilantro.

Cornflour: Cornstarch; thickening flour.

Curry: Often used in Vietnamese dishes but, unlike for Indian food, is not often mixed at home so use a good quality bought curry powder

Daikon: Oriental white radish, parsnip-shaped; use radishes.

Don ganh: bamboo pole for carrying goods on shoulders.

Dried shrimp: For making of shrimp sauce; shrimp paste is also an ingredient used in spicy dips and sauces.

Eggplant: Aka Chinese eggplant, thin and less bitter in Vietnam; rub with salt to draw out bitterness then wash if using plumper variety; also called aubergine

Fish sauce: Nuoc cham, pungent, salty, sauce made from fermented anchovies An essential ingredient in fish dipping sauce (nuoc cham). Keeps if indefinitely refrigerated.

Five spice Powder: Strong Chinese combo of Szechuan peppercorns, star anise, fennel, cloves and cinnamon; use sparingly.

Ginger: Has a refreshing scent, reminiscent of citrus, and a pleasant sharp flavour. Fresh, peeled, sliced, crushed, used in many dishes; powdered does not have same strong flavour

Hoisin sauce: Has a fragrant aroma with a rich, warm, sweet yet salty flavour. Chinese onion, black bean and garlic mix; ingredient or condiment.

Lemongrass: Has a distinctive citrus aroma with a intense lemon flavour, which has a hint of ginger. Lemony stalk to be bruised after discarding leaves.

Peeling: Available fresh, frozen, canned or dried.

Lychee: Juicy sweet fruit also dessert ingredient, grown prolifically.

Mushrooms: Straw most popular in Vietnam; substitute button or canned champignons; also dried wood or tree ear or dried black Chinese mushrooms to be soaked; dried not as flavoursome as fresh.

Mint: fresh ingredient or garnish; when combined chopped, equally with coriander, resembles *rau ram* (Vietnamese mint) aka polygonum.

Noodles: Dried cellophane or glass, from mung beans; reconstitute in hot water; fresh, wide noodles are used in pho soup; rice vermicelli, fresh or dry, doubles in quantity when cooked; dried or fresh Chinese yellow egg noodles are for soups and stir-fries.

Oyster sauce: Has a pleasant, fragrant aroma, and has a delicious and delicate flavour. thick mix of ground oysters, salt, water, cornflour and caramel, most used in stir-fries.

Papaya: Pawpaw; use green in salads; ripe orange colour, it's a sweet fruit.

Pho: National dish of beef noodle soup.

Pineapple: Use canned if fresh unavailable

Pork fat: Buy from butcher as its flavour cannot be replaced except by bacon fat

Rice: Vietnam's staple; long-grain accompanies sit-down meals; sticky rice is glutinous rice, sweeter and used as stuffing and in desserts.

Rice flour: basis for rice noodle and sweet dishes; cannot be substituted for glutinous rice; rice paper wrappers made from rice flour, commercially available, brittle and must be well dampened; see recipe under Appetisers.

Shrimps: See also dried shrimps; large shrimps are called prawns in some countries.

Spring onion: Aka shallot, scallion, green with white root, salad vegetable, ingredient and garnish.

Starfruit: Tropical tart fresh fruit also used in savory dishes.

Tet: Vietnamese new year; also name of other festivals with much eating

Turmeric: Has a peppery aroma with a hint of wood. It imparts a warm, slightly musky flavour. Yellow ochre coloured spice, used in curries and to add colour.

INDEX